This ~~~~~ dumb question but ...

How Does Money Work?

BY **JOE FAZIO**

ISBN-13: 978-1544871998
ISBN-10: 1544871996

Front cover image by Robb Helf

Co-authored and edited by Jack Henke

This book is dedicated to my family, who give me more love than one man deserves in a lifetime. You make me a better person. Thank you.

Table of Contents

PREFACE

How many times have you seen a shaky hand slowly raise and the first thing the brave hand-raiser nervously says is, "This might be a dumb question but . . .

You have a question. You look around the room. Are you the only one who doesn't understand? Does everyone else get it . . . except for you?

No. Everyone has the exact same question that you have, but they have another issue . . . *they're all afraid to ask.* Everyone in the room is waiting for someone else to ask the question that's been messing them up for years.

This is especially true when it comes to money. Take that feeling of embarrassment and multiply it by a thousand. Nobody teaches you about money. It's not taught in school. You would be amazed at how many accounting and finance school graduates do not know how money works.

It's not even taught at home, the place where you learn so many important things in life. If anything, talking about money is avoided. It's kept quiet, like a financial code of silence. When we were children, we learned that money has value. Parents, aunts, and uncles – our most trusted mentors, said, "Don't let anybody know how much money you have."

Yet, knowing how money works is one of the most important and least understood skills you can have in life.

You don't have to be rich to be happy, but you do have to have money. You don't have to raise your hand here. With this book, you will raise your understanding of money . . . easily.

If there were a class on money, you could raise your hand. There isn't one. Just read this book.

INTRODUCTION

The only way to make money problems go away is to understand money, how it works, and how to keep track of it.

How?

You may think, "Just give me more money and I won't have money problems." Really? How much money? *More money won't fix money problems unless you know how money works.* Don't get me wrong – more money might help, but it won't make your money problems go away.

Just ask anyone who once had money, but now is flat broke. It happens more than you think. Mike Tyson earned over $400 million in career boxing earnings. It's gone. Rapper 50 Cent (real name Curtis Jackson III) was ranked number 4 of the Forbes Fab 5 of wealthiest hip-hop stars in May 2015 with assets of $155 million. He declared bankruptcy the same year, and as Forbes wrote, "he may soon be worth less than his nickname."

These are unfortunate and spectacular falls from wealth, and there are many others. There are plenty of athletes, movie stars, lottery-winners and business owners who were riding high on a pile of cash that now have nothing. They don't know where it went.

If you understand your money, you will stop doing things you shouldn't do (like spending more than you have) and do things you should (like paying your bills on time).

The first question to ask is: "How does money work?"

That is the opposite of a dumb question. That is an incredibly smart question because most people don't understand it. Smart people. Not-so-smart people. It doesn't matter.

Money is everywhere. Think about it. You can get money electronically, manually, through ATMs, Mobile, Apple Pay, check, wire, People Pay (P2P), Green Dot, Bitcoin, and soon this list will be longer.

How does this make sense? Most people don't get it. That is why if they do get some money, they don't have it for long. You can't do anything with your money if you cannot find it. You can't invest it, spend or even blow it in Vegas if you can't find it first.

Think about your money like you are your money's parent. Not knowing where your child is causes panic. When you know where your children and your money are and that they are safe, you feel better. You feel less stressed. Your green babies are safe. You will find the same calmness in knowing where your money is, where it is coming from, and most importantly, where it is going.

This book is a red alert for your green.

Money is the #1 cause for stress in America. That's according to the American Psychological Association. 64% of Americans agree. Ask anybody. We all need to know where our money is.

So, if it's your money . . . where is it? Why is it so hard to know how much money you have and what you are doing with it?

Today, more than ever, we use the word money rather than cash. Not all that long ago, money was easy. Money was only cash. Cash is something you can hold or touch, like coins and bills. Cash is something you can hand to someone.

In addition to cash, money comes to you and leaves you in many ways, some of which we've already mentioned: through checks, mobile phones, credit cards, debit cards, prepaid cards, wires, person-to-person pay, Paypal, apps and more. You should know where your all of your money is . . . not just your cash.

The Internet should make tracking your money easier than ever. Like so many things about the Internet, it's a double-edged sword because it also makes it so much easier to spend.

Real money in real time can be a real problem.

How? You just need access to the Internet, and you can access your money. You can use a wired computer connection, WiFi, or a smartphone.

In Dr. Seuss's book *Green Eggs and Ham*, the main character (who interestingly is never named) describes everywhere he does not like green eggs and ham (which is anywhere). Your money is the opposite. You are not like a Dr. Seuss character... you do like your greenbacks, and you like them everywhere. We could almost call this book *Greenbacks and Ham*.

Cold hard cash does not have the same cache it used to carry. You cannot send cash (bills and coins) through the Internet and you should not even send it in the mail. You can do that with money because money is available in many different forms. If the person you need to give money to accepts it in the form you sent it, voilá you just used money in a form other than cash.

Voilá your money is everywhere, and voilá you are struggling to keep track of where it is. The cash is quicker than the eye.

When you send money somewhere, it is also important to understand the rules and costs of sending money in the form you selected, whether it is cash, check, Paypal, Apple pay, credit card, or debit card. That's important because sometimes your money leaves you in ways you don't expect.

You want to learn, but you don't want to spend much time doing it. I don't blame you. When it comes to spending either time or money, less is more.

Who am I? Why the heck should you listen to Joe Fazio, anyway?

Why listen to me? What knowledge, experience and training do I have? Well, I have an admission to make . . . I am one of those oddballs who have the background that qualifies me to talk about money.

Let me first say I did not start out with money, come from a wealthy family, or make millions overnight. I got out of college with debt, got married, bought a house, and had kids . . . just like many people do. I faced the same tough decisions about how much will I make, how much is my rent, mortgage, car payment, groceries, insurance, and all that stuff.

I have an undergraduate business degree and an MBA. These degrees helped me understand business, but it was really my interest in learning how to become rich (I'm still working on that) that helped me better understand money.

Over the last 30+ years of my life, I've found that I really do like to understand money and how it works in both my professional life and in my personal life. I like to keep things simple so I can understand them. And that's the way this book is written . . . simply.

So I have business degrees. Big deal. What else? Well, I worked as a salesperson for a big technology company (IBM) selling multi-million dollar deals. I've worked as a financial advisor holding securities and life insurance licenses (Northwestern Mutual). I've managed at a trust company and started a bank. I own laundromats, and have done lots of other investments in real estate and the stock market (some good, and some bad, really bad).

I've presented my ideas on money and how it works to elected state and federal government officials, to businesses, college classes and federal regulatory agencies. I know what I'm talking about. I've seen lots of money come and lots of money go . . . mine and others. I'm not the wealthiest guy in the world, but I've done okay.

Knowing where your money is and where it goes does not have to be a dream. You can make, and live confidently in, your financial bed. You can own it, too . . . if you take the first step.

We'll keep it simple.

Read on. You won't even have to raise your hand.

It's your money. Here's how it works . . .

CHAPTER 1

Money Makes Money. Money Costs Money.

There's an old joke about a thermos bottle that goes something like this: Did you know the thermos bottle is the greatest technological invention ever? You may think that many other inventions are much more advanced. What is so great about a thermos? A thermos bottle keeps hot stuff hot *and* cold stuff cold. So?

Well, how does it know when to do which one? Aha!

The same could be said for your money. Money costs money and makes money. It can do either, and it knows when to do which. It's really pretty simple. When you spend someone else's money, you need to pay them to use their money. What you pay is called *interest*. When you let someone else use your money, they pay you to use your money. This is also called interest. So money does both.

Once you understand that money costs money and money makes money, you will begin to make better money decisions.

If you feel you already know this and how to handle money, that is awesome. STOP READING THIS BOOK NOW. Give it to a friend, child, aunt, uncle, cousin, or coworker who needs to understand money. You are a good and valuable friend.

Do you remember the cartoon "Popeye?" There was a great character named Wimpy who often said, "I'll gladly pay you Tuesday for a hamburger today." Wimpy was always after instant gratification.

Imagine that on Wednesday, you and a buddy are together at McDonald's, staring at the dollar menu. Hamburgers are a buck. You have one dollar in your pocket and he has none. If he pulls a Wimpy and says to you, "I'll gladly pay you Tuesday for a hamburger today", what will your answer be?

Think about it: you get nothing now, while he gets a hamburger now. You won't have a dollar for a week (which is when he said

10

he was going to pay you, if he really does), so you don't get the pleasure of eating a burger for another week, while he gets the pleasure of eating the hamburger now. The only warm feeling you have in your stomach is that you helped out your friend. Try to digest that good feeling.

Would you loan him the dollar, putting off your benefit from your dollar for a week without getting something in return? If you said to him, "I'll give you my dollar for a burger, but you need to give me $1.10 on Tuesday," you just made a pretty good deal. Now you can have a hamburger next week, and a piece of candy. You got 10 cents for letting him use your dollar. Congratulations. You just made *interest*.

He paid 10 cents to use your dollar. He just paid interest. That is interesting… money both made money and money cost money in the same transaction, and it knew who to take interest from and to whom to pay it.

That's how money works. Except it really does not know who to take interest from and who to pay it to. Humans need to know that, and you need to be one of the humans that knows how it works.

Why?

The price for money varies from person to person and *borrower to borrower.*

The people who are most responsible with money pay less to use other people's money. Less responsible people pay more. How? By the amount of interest being charged.

In our example above (excluding a lot of other factors that are not important right now), your friend paid 10% interest, as 10% of one dollar = 10 cents. If you pay 10 cents to use a dollar, (which is worth 100 cents) then you paid 10% in interest because $10 \div 100 = 10\%$.

If your friend had repaid you $1.05 for the use of a dollar, they would have paid 5% in interest, as 5% of one dollar = 5 cents $(5 \div 100 = 5\%)$.

"Big deal," you may scoff. "A nickel? Who cares?" Don't scoff so fast. When you are working with real money for real things, like borrowing $100,000 for a home, paying 5% vs. 10% is quite a difference. In a year, 5% interest costs you $5,000. 10% interest costs you $10,000.

That's a difference of $5,000!

That's real money to anyone. You could have an extra $5,000 for a vacation, or pay $5,000 in interest. It's not a trick question. It is an easy choice.

Make money work for you . . . not cost you.

CHAPTER 2

Why are Credit Cards like Power Tools?

Power Tools are so cool. Man, even the name sounds good. Let's talk about power tools. Why? Power tools make jobs easier. And to be honest, some people just get a charge out of using them. Power tools can be, well, empowering.

When you buy your kid a bike, they get a big thrill . . . once it's assembled. Which tool would you rather use – a regular screwdriver or a power screwdriver? Which one will make a much quicker job out of it? The power drill makes drilling holes much easier. The power saw makes it much faster to cut boards than a handsaw and it makes straighter cuts. A snow blower is faster at clearing snow and easier (particularly on your back) to use than a shovel. A power lawnmower is faster than an old manual push mower. Ever see a carpenter use a nail gun? Talk about speed, not to mention all the fingers that were spared the hammer. Speed and efficiency – you get the idea.

What is it that makes power tools so valuable? They save time. Time is the ultimate limited resource. You can never get it back. Power tools make it easier to do a job. They do the work more effectively than we could do it without them.

Can power tools cause problems? You bet they can. How badly can you cut yourself with a handsaw? You can make a nice slice but it won't be too bad in the long run. The worst case is you might need a stitch or two. How badly can you hurt yourself with a power saw? You can easily cut off a finger, or even your hand. Stitches would be minor. You can cause enough damage to require surgical repair. Any scar will certainly last a lifetime.

It's the same with a power lawn mower, snow blower or any other power tool. They all pack power and capability, but you really need to know how to operate any one of them properly to be safe.

The power can be potentially, and easily, dangerous.

When it comes to using money, credit cards are power tools. They even make it very easy to spend money you do not have, and they do it very effectively. With the swipe of a card, you can spend lots of money, lots of times, every day.

Even easier – load the card on your smartphone. Now you don't even have to carry the card! Proceed with extreme caution – it now has the same power tool capabilities.

Boy, it's helpful to have that card. You don't need to go to the bank to get cash. You don't need to write or cash a check, and you don't need to go to the ATM to get cash. You just swipe your card. Now that's power. Just think of all that time and effort you saved spending money.

What's the problem? Just like real power tools, credit cards can cause more and worse harm than a manual tool. The buying power that a credit card provides can be just as dangerous as a power tool. The cuts can be deep and serious.

When you use a credit card, *you are actually borrowing money every time you use it.*

This is true even if you pay off the entire balance before the end of each month.

Credit cards do a lot of good things. Needing to get cash each time you wanted to purchase something would get old and time-consuming. So would the worry about carrying around too much cash for fear of loss or theft.

That card, oh, that beautiful card. That's all anyone needs. You don't need to count money, keep track of money, worry about not having enough money for the next purchase, go get money, or make sure you have the right change. Just swipe and go. The credit card company will keep track of everything for you.

Because it is so easy, your charges add up fast. The statement comes and you can't pay the full amount you owe. So you make a payment, which the credit card company happily accepts and charges you interest for using their money.

The next month comes and you have the same problem . . . you can't pay the full balance, only now it's last month's balance and this month's balances that you cannot pay. So you make a payment. The credit card company adds more interest fees to your balance. The money you borrowed is piling up on you in a negative way. You keep owing more money and paying less. It is not a formula for success.

The negative cash pile is actually a hole. Why is this a bigger problem than running out of cash? When you run out of cash, you are out. You can't spend more than you have. In fact, if you have any sense at all, you will slow down or stop your spending when you realize you are running low.

Now, you may not be able to buy all of the things you want like designer clothes, cool cars, or sadly, power tools. Nor can you dine out in restaurants, and go to concerts, sporting events, etc. Yeah, I know, that's the fun stuff. When you've run out of cash and you cannot afford things you want or like, or maybe even need, it's like cutting yourself with a handsaw. It's not going to kill you, or even scar you really badly for life. Sure, it hurts a little. You will heal.

You should be able to do the same with a credit card. Stop spending before you spend more than you can pay off in a month (just like running out of cash). Many people do. It's the people who don't track their charges and are then unable to pay the full balance that get into trouble.

How much trouble? They keep going backwards because charging more items increases the balance you owe and the interest costs continue to mount. The negative cash pile is becoming a bigger hole. At some point you can't pay enough each month to reduce the balance you owe. In fact, you can't make what they call the minimum payment.

Now your credit rating falls due to late payments or no payment at all. They are likely to cut off your credit card, too. All the power is lost.

You may have other payments to make each month: car, house,

student loan, etc. If you decide to pay more on the credit card and not make one of the other payments, you'll face more problems, and get more bad marks against your credit. If you miss three payments on your house, you may have to deal with foreclosure (that is bad). If you miss too many car payments, your car will be taken away from you (repossessed, or "repo'd" as the professionals call it).

You don't have enough money to make all the payments you have to make, and you still need to eat, maintain your home and car, wash your clothes, and more. What happens? You declare bankruptcy. You work through a complex legal process to get those to whom you owe money to forgive your mistake and say they won't make you pay. That may seem like a good answer. You got to spend a bunch of other people's money and you never had to pay them back. In reality, it is not a good answer.

One of the things that comes along with bankruptcy is the loss of financial power tools for several years. It takes about seven years to wipe out a bankruptcy. You will struggle to get credit of any kind, and when you do, it will be very costly because you will pay higher rates of interest.

Without power tools like credit cards, you are back to living on cash. That may help you stay out of trouble from overspending, but you lose all the efficiency and effectiveness of the power tools. You spend much more time just doing transactions, paying bills, and managing finances.

In this case, you've cut yourself seriously from a financial standpoint. It will badly scar you for a long time, if not for life. Foolishly spending money you don't have without regard for your ability to make payments on it and your other obligations puts you in a deep hole. Climbing out of this hole is difficult and can take a very long time.

How do you use credit cards wisely? Only charge as much as you can completely pay off at the end of each month. If you can pay $1,000, you can charge $1,000. If it is $500, don't charge more than that.

If you follow this advice, you do not pay any interest. You get to use "OPM" – Other People's Money – for a short window of time. That is really cool.

How do you figure that out? See how much money you have left after paying all of your other obligations each month. That is what you have left for food, entertainment, savings, gas, and new toys. Basically, anything else you can spend money on.

Now, if you don't want to figure that out, here's an easier way. It's called, "Living within your means." Making good choices. How do you do that? It's easy, but it can be hard. Look around. When you get invited to go out with your friends or co-workers at a hot new spot, ask yourself if you can afford to spend the $50 (at least) that it will cost. Instead, what if you got a little creatively cost-conscious? You could invite them to your place, and get everyone involved by having them bring a dish to pass while you supply the refreshments. The result: you come off as a fun host who knows how to throw a party (while you save a few bucks).

There are lots of examples like this we could go through. Here's just one more. Where do you shop for clothes? Do you buy only those things that are on sale? Do you buy quality and value or do you buy designer to impress yourself or others?

One other important factor about credit cards is the interest rates they charge. Basically, they are high rates for everyone. Chapter 15 explains how higher interest rates cost you more money. Credit cards are one of the most expensive ways to borrow money if you're not paying off the balance every month.

Just because you can swipe the card to charge something does not mean you can afford it or should afford it. *Think about how you would spend your money if you were paying with cash.* That's how you should think about using your credit card. Don't change your spending and shopping habits just because you can swipe a card. You must still pay for what you charged. If not with actual money, you will pay with your reputation, your ability to use credit, and ultimately, how you will be able to live your life.

The smart question is, "Why trade charging a little short-term fun for keeping the power for the long run?"

Keep your power.

CHAPTER 3

Why is a Debit Card the Other Power Tool?

You're thinking, "Wait, in the last chapter you told me that credit cards are the power tools of money. Now you are calling the debit card a power tool. How can that be?"

Just like using a credit card, using a debit card is easy.

Remember how we defined a power tool - they are very effective at making jobs easier. They save time. They do the work more effectively, better than we could do without them. We call them power tools because they give us lots of power and capability. Power tools also come with a warning - You really need to know how to operate them properly in order to safely use them.

You have to respect a power tool . . . the power, how to handle it, and the potential danger.

How is a debit card different from a credit card? First, a debit card does not provide you with credit and give you the ability to spend money you never had. Debit cards are another way to access money you have in your bank account. There are several ways to access your money: write a check, show up in person to withdraw money, ask the bank to wire it, use an ATM (Automated Teller Machine) with your card, via a mobile app, online banking, or use your debit card at a store. More methods are being invented every day.

Of all the ways to access money in your account, the debit card is very convenient, fast, and easy. Naturally, the speed and ease also make debit cards so dangerous. The easy access to cash (or power) can cause problems of a different nature for you. With credit cards, the danger is borrowing money to spend and then being eaten alive by interest payments.

With debit cards, the danger is how much it costs you when you so easily access cash you think you have . . . but don't really have. Remember, nothing is free.

A debit card works like any other withdrawal from your checking account. When you write a check, when it goes through processing, and the bank subtracts the money from your account and deposits it into someone else's account – the person or business to whom you wrote the check. With checks, this might take a couple of days.

The same is true for a debit card . . . except it's faster. Once you swipe/touch your debit card and sign your name or enter your personal code to confirm the transaction, you should think that the money is coming out of your account and going into the other's account at that exact moment.

What's the big deal?

Speed kills.

Banks issue you a checkbook so you can write checks to others to transfer money from you to them. The bank gives you a tool to allow you to freely make payments, but they don't follow you around looking at the balance in your account before you write every check. The bank does not tell you not to write a check that is for more money than you have in your account.

That's on you.

The bank assumes you will be a responsible user of the tool and only write checks when you know you have money in your account. When that check goes through the processing cycle and is presented to your bank for payment, if they see that you do not have enough money in your account, they take one of the following actions:

1. They return the check to the person you gave it to saying you do not have enough funds to cover the check. The bank then charges you a fee for violating the terms of your account and for the extra processing time and cost they have incurred.

Now the person with your bad check is going to hound you for what you owe them. You can't blame them, because, well, you owe them.

2. They cover the check for the amount you wrote, contact you to come and make a deposit to cover the check and charge you a fee. If you're lucky enough to get this treatment, you won't be hounded by the person to whom you wrote the check.

3. They provide you with a service called overdraft protection. It automatically sets up a loan for you to cover the amount of the check and you now have a loan to repay. You don't pay an overdraft fee, but for this to be a real alternative for you, you must have this service set up prior to any overdrafts, usually when you open the account. No hounding here either, but know that once again, you are really borrowing money and paying interest.

4. If you are a really good client, and you have never had an overdraft before (or it's been years since your last one), they might cover the overdraft for you, call you to come in and make a deposit, and waive the fee. This option does not happen very often.

Okay, so now that you understand what happens with a check, how is it different than a debit card? At the start, it actually works the same. The bank issues you a debit card assuming you will be a responsible user of the tool. No one follows you around looking at your account balance for you each time you are about to access your money using your debit card. Everything else speeds up from there.

Let's set up a little scenario. Payday is a couple of days away. You think you have $100 in your account so you use your debit card for the following purchases:

1. Perfect Cup of Coffee $4

2. McAdoo's lunch $10

3. High Octane Gas $25 (hey, your car has a small tank)

4. Harry's Hardware $30 (lawn fertilizer and toilet repair parts)

Total $69

The problem comes in when you really don't have $100 left in your account. Why might that be? You forgot to subtract a check or debit transaction from your account. You added wrong after your last deposit. You subtracted wrong after a withdrawal. Maybe you never bother to track your balance anyway and just keep track, or you think you do, in your mind. Maybe you just don't care. The point is you actually had $0 in your account before you made the four debit purchases listed above.

Why is that bad?

First – you spent money you did not have. This is a bad habit to start.

Second – you violated the terms of your account agreement.

Third – it all happened pretty fast.

Every time you spend money that you don't have in your account, you incur an overdraft charge. Let's assume that's $30. Add $30 to each of your purchases above and you bought a $34 cup of coffee, $40 fast food lunch, $55 of gas (that's about $7/gallon) and $60 worth of toilet parts and fertilizer. Total cost $189. Hope that cup of coffee was really good.

You would get real angry if you were charged four overdraft fees, but if you overdraft, that is the price you pay. I've seen this happen with college students who have a debit card for the first time, and their parents are the ones who get mad because the bank keeps charging for overdrafts and the kid just does not get it or care to get it.

I have a friend who told me this tale of woe – his college-age son had 12 overdrafts in one month and the debit card was terrible. And the damn bank kept charging fees. I asked if his son understood how the card worked. His response was no. I asked if he explained to his son how it worked. His response; "No, I've never had a debit card."

Duh. He didn't even understand how they work. He just wanted to be mad at someone. The point? This should be a tale of "Whoa!" instead of a tale of woe.

You can quickly pile up overdraft charges with the debit card, *effectively increasing the cost of many of the things you buy.* You are spending money you don't have. You are overpaying.

Debit cards are not all bad. Used wisely, a debit card is a useful banking power tool. If you have one, you don't have to carry around cash or a checkbook or worry about running out of either cash or checks. Debit cards also allow you to withdraw money from an ATM.

When you're traveling, good luck trying to find someone to cash a check. It's nearly impossible if you are buying something, and even more so if you are not. Even then, you better have plenty of identification and prove your check will be "good." Finally, debit cards are much less risky than carrying lots of cash with you.

The next time you're going to use your debit card, think about the word *swipe*. When you swipe your card, you're instantly swiping that money from your account. If your card has a chip in it, remember to keep some of your chips in the bank. Keep track of how much you have and you keep the power.

More (debit) power to you.

CHAPTER 4

Why is it Easier to Save a Dollar than to Make a Dollar?

There's an old saying, "It's easier to save a dollar than it is to make a dollar." How does that work? Don't you need to have the dollar first, before you can save it?

Well, actually, no. In our upcoming example of using a credit card to purchase something that you can save $500 on, you don't really have the $500. Remember, every time you use your credit card, you are borrowing money. You don't have the money. The key is to pay the full balance owed on the card every month to avoid interest payments. It pays to think of your credit card monthly bill as a short-term loan. Paying it off effectively pays off that short-term loan made to you. You did not use your money to make the purchases, you used someone else's, (the company or bank that issued the credit card to you). If you do not pay it in full, you have to pay interest charges.

They would prefer you pay less than the balance each month, so they can charge you interest. In this example, we're going against the grain on the advice to pay off the balance each month.

Maybe it takes you three months to pay it off. But hey, you are saving $500. It has to be a real $500, not just a ½ price item that you would like to have. No, this is something you needed and intended to buy, and you've found it at a bargain price.

So, if it costs you $10 per month in interest charges for 3 months, you spent $30 in interest. You still saved $470 ($500 − $30 =$470). Not bad. By charging it, you are still way ahead of the game.

Did you really save more money? Yes. It's easier to save a dollar than to make a dollar. Here's why. If you earn $500 per week in your job, you don't get to keep all $500. Why not?

First, there are taxes. Let's assume you pay 10% of your wages in taxes. That costs you $50 ($500 x 10% = $50). Before you get paid, you're down to $450. Now, to be able to make $500, you need to get to/from work. You drive 10 miles each way and your car gets 20 miles per gallon. Gas costs $3 per gallon. One gallon per day for 5 days is $15. You are now down to $435. You eat lunch each day that's $3/day (hey, you take your lunch to work each day), that's another $15; you're down to $420. The list goes on: clothes for work, insurance, daycare if you have kids, car maintenance, etc. Let's just say it adds up to another $20/week.

You now have $400. It cost you $100 to make $500, leaving you $400. So, was it easier to make $500 or save $500?

Answer: Saving $500 was much easier.

When you think of it that way, saving might not be as painful as you think.

CHAPTER 5

Everyone Spends Their Money Differently. Why?

Credit your sources. Give credit where credit is due. Giving people the credit they deserve is important. So, the credit for this chapter goes to my dad. This exists only because my dad shared his knowledge with me. So, thanks Dad. He shared his name with me… and a whole lot more. Now I can share his wisdom with you.

Everybody spends their money differently.

Rule Number One: You cannot keep up with everyone when it comes to spending money. Nor do you want to. If you do, it's likely you will end up broke. You will own lots of stuff that does not bring you any fun, happiness, or contentment.

Why would you want to do that?

I'm not saying you should not spend money on the things you enjoy. Just make sure the things you choose to spend your money on are the things that you enjoy. Many people get caught up spending money on things other people really like, only to find out they really don't like other people's things that much.

What am I talking about? Name it – jewelry, boats, shoes, cars, designer clothes and purses, timeshares, motorcycles, four-wheelers, horses, snowmobiles, travel, artwork, furniture, dining, bicycles, collectibles, antiques, sports equipment, guns, season tickets, etc.

Now, I do own a boat. In fact, I've owned one since 1986. Currently, I'm on my third one, which makes just three boats in 28 years. I owned my second boat for 17 years.

Yes, I cleverly rationalized my way to purchasing a new boat when the old one worked fine. However, I really enjoy boating and watersports. My family does, too.

When I tell someone I bought a new boat, they ask me why. I just love that.

Or they tell me that I wasted my money. I love that even more. Or they may share with me that my next happiest day will be the day I sell the boat.

I don't think so. Boating is my thing and I love it. That does not mean I want a boat like yours. I want a boat that works best for small, inland lakes and water sports and the occasional slow, evening cruise. We have a cottage on shore so I don't need a huge cruiser. It's on a small lake so we can easily get to the cottage if we forget something or need to use the facilities.

Now, if I had seen a friend's boat that is 30 feet long and is used on the Great Lakes for fishing and thought, "Wow that's cool," would I go buy it? No. I have fun fishing or going out for a nice ride on the Great Lakes, but I'd find it boring doing that on a regular basis. It is not right or wrong. It is just not for me.

It's the same with really expensive golf equipment and a membership at a country club. I like to golf, but not that much. Club membership is just not that important to me. Different strokes, you know?

Lots of things are like that in my life, and in your life, too. You have to decide how to spend your own money. Be yourself. Your money can help you be yourself, too. Express yourself. Invest in yourself.

So when it comes down to it, the why is easy . . . everybody spends their money differently because everybody is different.

And thanks Dad.

CHAPTER 6

What Do You Choose to Afford?

We all make choices. Some are good. Some are not so good. We are human. There is no getting away from that. I wish every decision I made was good, but it just does not happen. As long as you can make more good choices than bad, and the bad ones are not too terribly bad, you should be okay. Don't be too hard on yourself.

When is comes to money, it's no different. Some decisions you make are better than others. A long time ago, I started my first job out of college. My starting salary was $21,900 per year. This first job was not going to make me rich, but, hey, I felt rich.

Why? Before that job, I had never made more than about $3,000 per year in my life. Summer jobs, part-time jobs, grants, scholarships, and student loans got me through college. Before that I was kid number five in a family of eight kids. There was no real money there, either.

So, with my first job, I was making seven times more than my previous highest income for one year. Man, I was flush.

The reason I'm telling you all this because once I started my job, I found myself among a collection of co-workers of varying ages, all of whom seemed to have more money and higher incomes than me. And for the most part, that was true.

What I noticed was that the people I worked and hung around with all drove nicer cars than me. Remember the previous chapter, everybody spends their money differently.

I am not repeating myself here. It took me awhile to figure it out. Somewhere along the line I did realize everybody spends their money differently and I needed to make choices with my money to buy things that I valued, not what others did.

My first job taught me that you can choose not to afford something. Once I got my financial feet under me - understanding what my expenses were, paying bills on time, and saving a little money, I had more money to spend on stuff.

When I would talk with friends and co-workers who were in a similar financial situation to mine, I would talk about how the others all seemed to buy expensive cars. I figured out that with my increasing income that I could afford a nice new car, too. I chose not to do it.

As I talked with my friends about earning, saving, spending and investing money, I would say, "I can afford to drive a new Cadillac. I choose not to afford one." That was a long time ago, when a Cadillac was *the* car. Today, that might be a new Lexus.

Anyway, at the time, I bought a Pontiac (I don't think they make them any longer) and still saved money. Eventually, I was also able to buy a small boat and I spent less on those two items than other people spent on just one car.

The point is about making money choices. Even though your income allows you to spend money on something, it does not mean you have to spend money on something. Even though you can afford a nice new car, it does not mean you need to buy one.

Why not? Well, that is your choice. You can choose to spend more or you can choose to spend less. Choosing does not automatically mean spending more. You can choose to spend less.

When I chose not to buy a more expensive car, it was because I saw a better path for me. Drive a decent car, and continue to save (and ultimately invest) money. I was making better choices for me. Sure I could choose to afford a fancy car, but I chose not to do it. Sometimes you can choose the road less traveled in a decent car.

When it comes to life insurance, another money-based product, there are many different strategies from which to choose. One popular strategy is, "Buy term and invest the difference." Term life insurance premiums (payments) are cheaper than those for permanent life insurance, but permanent life insurance builds up cash value like other investments. Some planners would tell you to buy term insurance and invest the difference in premiums (payments), with the logic being you can make more money on other investments than on permanent life insurance.

Ah, we're back to choices. You may think, "Hey, if I pay $200 per month less in life insurance premiums, I can invest $200 per month."

The catch with that theory is most people make a different choice, like buying a new car, for example. The new car comes with a new monthly payment, so there are no savings there. If you bought term life insurance and a new car, you chose to not build money in a permanent life insurance policy or in any other investments.

There are no judgments . . . just choices.

What will make you feel better - knowing how you spend your money and having some 'in the bank' or choosing to show to everyone else how you spend your money?

We'll talk about that next.

CHAPTER 7

What is a Payment Buyer?

You may be a car buyer, a homebuyer or a college education buyer. What you don't want to be is a payment buyer. A payment buyer (this is another one of my dad's gems) comes at buying things differently. A payment buyer thinks because they are "used to making a payment" they will just keep making them.

Some of the people we discussed in the last chapter are payment buyers. Now think about that for a minute. Would you rather be used to making a $400 per month car payment and have to keep making that payment forever? Or would you prefer to stop making a $400 per month payment (even if only for a month or two) and keep $400 per month?

Take the money? Give away the money? It's just $400. Are you kidding me?

Hmm, I don't know about you, but I would choose to keep $400 per month every time.

A payment buyer doesn't typically think about the useful life of the item or the rate they are paying for the money (interest). That's right . . . *keep in mind the rate you're paying to use the money.* Always remember that you will pay to use the money (interest).

The payment buyer's thought process is "I have a $400 per month car payment. I want a new car. I'm going to trade my car in at the new car dealer. They have a real nice, red SUV that I want. Even though I have 2 ½ years to go on my loan, they can take the balance on it, loan me money for the new car, stretch it over 7 years for me, and keep my payment at $400." Done deal dot com.

It's a great deal. Maybe. Or maybe not so much.

Voilá . . . that is the magic of payment buying! Only it's not magic. It's voodoo. And voodoo is usually bad.

What this translates into is making payments for another four and a half years. Reread that last sentence and let it sink in for a moment.

Four and a half years.

It is not usually a good idea. If you do this, you are stretching out your loan. Often, it happens when you get bored with the car you bought. It can happen faster than you think.

More importantly, once you start payment buying and you see a beautiful new car, it's easy to get hooked. If you do it today, you are likely to do it again, and sooner than you think. In fact, payment buyers usually do it with everything they buy on credit- even credit cards. They don't worry about the balance that is accumulating. They just focus on making the monthly payment they are used to making, whether that is $100, $200, $300 or more.

It doesn't matter if someone owes $1,000 or $10,000, they get used to making a payment. So they just keep doing it.

Take control of your financial life. You owe it to yourself. It's up to you. Be a smart buyer, not a payment buyer. Your financial quality of life will feel even better than a rad, new red car.

Rock on.

CHAPTER 8

A Ton of Steel or a Ton of Dollars?

There is an old riddle that goes like this, "What weighs more – a ton of steel or a ton of feathers?"

Most people answer a ton of steel, thinking of course that steel is heavy and feathers are light. They are right, a piece of steel is heavier than a feather. However, a ton is 2,000 pounds, and whether you are weighing feathers, steel, potatoes, or sand, 2,000 pounds of something still weighs 2,000 pounds. It just takes a lot more feathers to get there than steel.

We are asking the same question with money. Yes, from a weight perspective, a ton is a ton. What if the ton of steel is a car and the ton of money is your bank account?

What would you rather have, a cool car that impresses people who think, "Wow that Joe is an amazing guy, just look at the car he drives." Or, when you pull up next to amazing Joe in his cool car, does it make you feel like you just don't have the money he does? It makes you feel kinda, sorta inferior in a way.

When you know where your money is and you are confident you know how to use it well, neither an amazing Joe nor an ordinary Joe will ever make you feel inferior. You know how you manage, save, and spend your money. Why would what someone else has make you feel bad?

It doesn't when you understand money.

Understanding your money is like having an amazing superpower. Pulling up next to amazing Joe and his cool car will have no effect on you. In fact, it will have the opposite effect. You are likely to think he is a payment buyer with payments to make for many years on a car that is worth less than he owes on it.

You, on the other hand, know you spent less on a car but (for once, this is a good but) you have $10,000 in the bank. How does that make you feel? It makes me feel much better. I know how I spend my money, and I know how I save money. If you do, you will be comfortable as well.

More money + less payments = less stress

So, which would you rather have: $10,000 of steel or $10,000 of money? Superman was the man of steel. You can be a person of made of feathers and it won't make Superman any stronger than you. Your superpower of knowing how money works will let you handle a ton of anything.

CHAPTER 9

Coffee, Tea . . . or Vacation?

Guilty pleasures, habits (good or bad), simple indulgences, and lack of willpower... we all have to deal with these. They are just different for everyone. One thing that is the same for all of us is that these things usually cost money. Let's use a simple example of coffee.

How would you even attempt to count the number of people that cannot live without their favorite coffee? There are so many choices: Starbucks, Seattle's Best, Dunkin Donuts, McDonald's or your favorite local coffee shop, etc.

Many people, and I do mean many, purchase a cup of coffee every day. I'm not talking about those that treat themselves to a cup occasionally; I'm talking about the "every-dayers".

Coffee is really pretty cheap when you buy coffee grounds or beans and make it yourself at home. It likely costs less than $.50 a day (for more than one cup). So, why spend $4 per day on coffee? Do that 5 times a week on your way to work and you've spent $20. In seven days a week it will cost you $28. In a year's time, you've spent over $1,000 on coffee.

I know, you're saying, "But I like their coffee, and it is my only indulgence." If you can afford it, and you choose to spend your money on it, good for you. My point here is many people simply do not realize the amount of money they are spending on something simple that can be purchased much more cheaply. Insert your indulgence of choice here: lunch at home vs. lunch in a restaurant, soda from a 12 pack at home vs. from a convenience store or fast food restaurant.

Whether you are spending money on soda or cigarettes, you are spending money. It is not a moral or ethical judgment. It is a financial judgment. You are making it. No one else is.

Would you prefer a $1,200 vacation? People spend money on

simple things like this all the time. Then they wonder why they don't have money or complain they would like to go on a vacation but they can't afford it.

If that cup of coffee every day is preventing you from saving money for a vacation (or emergency fund, retirement, home, education for your kids, or anything else you'd like to have money for) then you just found your source of money to build that whatever-you-want-or-need fund.

You don't even have to skip your indulgence or habit all the time, or forever. Treat yourself once a week. Learn about compound interest (next chapter) and start saving now, then let your money work for you.

In a few years, you just might be able to afford, choose to afford, and enjoy whatever your daily indulgence is and still have money saved for other purposes.

This is like found money. It will deliver a bigger jolt than a double espresso. Cheers!

CHAPTER 10

What is Compound Interest?

The math here is simple. In fact, we'll do all of it for you. In order to make good decisions you need to really understand compound interest. It sounds complicated, but it's really simple.

It is also very powerful. If you don't believe it, listen to the smartest man who ever lived. Albert Einstein said, "Compound interest is the most powerful force in the universe." He referred to it as the eighth wonder of the world. He said, "He who understands it, earns it . . . he who doesn't . . . pays it."

Money makes money or money costs money.

There has been some argument about whether Einstein actually said these things. Regardless, it's wise to have compound interest work for you and not against you. Make your money work for you.

What does that really mean?

We can skip the math below if you simply understand that money grows faster if the interest on it is greater. You can get returns on money by investing it in something that grows in value like the stock market, or by earning interest on your money like you would earn from a bank in a savings account or a certificate of deposit.

If you really understand that and how powerful it is to get a greater rate of return, you will see why compound interest is so powerful.

Let me do a little simple math to make my point. If you earn 4% interest, your money will double in 18 years. Sounds like a long time, but remember your money is working for you.

What happens if you earn 8% instead of 4%? Your money doubles in just 9 years. That's just half the time it takes at 4%.

You may say, "Big deal. Nine years is still a long time." Yes it is, but if you could find your way to saving $10,000 by age 30, let's look at what happens by the time you are just 65 years old:

Age	4% Return on $10,000	8% Return on $10,000
39	$14,233	$20,000
48	$20,000	$40,000
57	$28,466	$80,000
66	$40,000	$160,000

Which amount would you rather have at age 66 or any point along the way?

There are a few things to notice here:

Even though the 4% rate is half of the 8% rate, your money grows by less than half in the same time periods (at age 39 it grew by $10,000 @ 8%; but only by $4,233 @ 4%). At a 4% interest over the same number of years, the money only doubled twice, but at 8% it doubled 4 times!

At the same rate of return over the same time period, money doubles, regardless of the actual dollar amount; $10,000 to $20,000 or $80,000 to $160,000 (yes, it works at higher numbers: $1 million to $2 million).

Most importantly, start saving now so your money can work for you longer. Regardless of when you start saving, the doubling you miss out on is the last one. The biggest one. That is really important to understand. You never miss out on the first doubling. You always miss out on the last doubling. The first one has to happen first before the next one can happen. And the next one. And the next one . . .

Here's a compounding and confounding irony: You never miss out on the first one, which is why most people don't get started in the first place.

The people who miss out think, "Big deal. I work to save $10,000 and it doubles to $20,000." What they should think is, "I'm missing out on $80,000 by not starting now!"

This is one reason why people say the first million you make is the toughest. Once you build a pile of money, it starts working for you. Your income will also increase over your lifetime, giving you more money to put in savings and making it easier to have another million.

Here's an easy math trick to determine how long it will take your money to double at a given rate of return. It's called the rule of 72. If you divide the number 72 by the rate of return you expect to receive, the result will be the number of years it takes for your money to double:

Rate of Return / 72 = Years to Double
72 / 2% = 36 Years
72 / 4% = 18 Years
72 / 6% = 12 Years
72 / 8% = 9 Years

It works with any number. It even works in reverse. If you want to know what rate of return you need to double your money in a given number of years; divide 72 by the number of years and the result will be the rate of return it will take. 72/9 years = 8%; 72/4 years = 18%.

Is it realistic to earn 8% on a CD? Yes, it could happen. In the next 30 years, bank rates will change. If you don't believe me, consider this – from 1984 to 2014, interest rates varied from just over 12% to just under 1%. Rates do change. Stock market returns fluctuate every year, every day, and even every hour.

Compound interest really is powerful stuff. I think I believe Einstein. He was a pretty smart guy, no question about it.

CHAPTER 11

Who Is the Boss? Make that Money Work for You.

Have you ever heard the saying, "Make your money work for you"? Ever wonder what the heck that means? You think, "I have a job and I work for my money."

The truth is that most of us, if not all of us, have to work to get some money before we can get money to work for us. Get a job, make some money, and live on less money than you make. Get some money saved in the bank and in your 401(k) for retirement.

So, you are working for a living. You need to save. If you do, you can get money working for you. Here's how:

You save money . . . a few bucks for an emergency fund, bigger purchases, vacations, etc. It earns interest in a bank account. That money is working for you, and it will be there when you need it. Make sure you save enough for a down payment on a house. Houses generally (although not always) go up in value. That money is working for you.

You contribute to your 401(k) through automatic withdrawals from your paycheck. If you don't know what a 401(k) is, ask your employer to explain it to you. Your 401(k) is likely invested in the stock market, and that money is working for you. Remember, it starts out slowly. Stay the course. Money doubles. It's the last doubling you'll miss out on, not the first one. The last doubling is the biggest.

If you have a child, start saving for their education when they are young. Start the day they are born or the day you get their social security number. There are special college education savings accounts called 529 plans. Look it up online and start one. That money will be invested and working for you and for your child. What if your kid doesn't go to college, or better yet, gets scholarships to go to college?

Whoopie! You still have the money you saved.

Okay, now you have a little money saved in your emergency, vacation, and whatever else fund. You can spend it. Remember that car you like? You don't need it, but you sure would like it. Are payments to be made on it in addition to the down payment from your savings? No thanks.

What if you used some of the money you saved to invest? Then you'd have more money working for you. It's not all that hard to get money working for you. It takes some discipline, and a willingness to invest rather than spend.

Don't invest all your money. You need to enjoy life, too. This is one way to look at it - if you get your money working for you now, you'll be surprised at how happy you'll be later. You will have even more money to spend.

What's the secret? Work for some money. Save some to get it working for you. It's like having a second job without punching the clock for it.

Now *that's* what I call working. You are the boss.

Read on to learn more about how this all works . . . for you.

CHAPTER 12

How Does Money Get a Raise?

Your money is working for you. You have it in a bank account earning interest, invested in the stock market, invested through a 401(k) or IRA, or anywhere else you are being paid for the use of your money.

That's right – you are being paid for the use of your money!

The beauty of having money working for you is that it never needs a vacation. It only takes a break when you take it out to spend it. If it is not in an account earning interest or making a return, then it is on vacation.

When you think about it, money should get a raise for all the years of service it is providing you in those accounts, just like employees do. The good news is money does get raises. Here's how:

Remember we talked about the value of compound interest, the Rule of 72, and that the doubling you miss out on is always the last one, never the first one? I'm combining all three of those concepts into one simple example.

First, let's use a simple rate of return that divides evenly into 72; that would be 8%. 72/8% means your money doubles in 9 years. If you've saved $10,000 by age 25; at an 8% return, your money would double to $20,000 in 9 years. The chart below shows how your money grows:

Age	Account Balance
25	$10,000
34	$20,000
43	$40,000
52	$80,000
61	$160,000
70	$320,000

There are 3,285 days in a nine year period (365 x 9). During the first nine year period, when your money doubles from $10,000 to $20,000, it is earning an average of about $3.04 per day.

During the last nine-year period, when your money doubles from $160,000 to $320,000, your money is earning about an average of $48.70 per day. That is sixteen times more than during the first doubling period.

Now, that's a nice raise. And remember, your money is not working any harder or any more hours to do that. Neither are you. That's the best part.

Will it turn out exactly as presented here? Will you earn 8% on all your money? Will it be an even 8% every year? Is it really the same amount every day? No, of course not. What is really important to understand about money is that when you get your money working for you, and it grows, you start making more money just by it growing. The bigger the account balance, the more you make (at the same rate of interest or return).

Don't believe me yet? Let's try this example, which is also true. You will ask yourself, "How can it be?"

You start saving money at age 25. You save $2,000 per year for 10 years (by saving $166.67 per month), and then you stop saving. That's right… you stop saving. You actually contributed only $20,000 to the account, but at the end of 10 years of saving, your account has about $30,750 in it (your deposits plus interest). Then you stopped saving. You are 35 years old. At the same rate of return as above, 8%, at age 70 you will have $500,000.

What happens if you wait until age 35 to start saving? You start saving $2,000 per year (by saving $166.67/month) earning 8%. One major difference is you decide to save $2,000 per year until age 70. That's 35 years of saving, not just 10. You probably figure that even though you waited to start saving, you will save more because you never stopped saving.

Not true. Your account at age 70 only grew to $382,000, much less than if you started saving ten years earlier. Why? When you wait to start saving, you simply do not allow your money to get as many raises.

By the way, in the example that started saving at 25 and then stopped, you only put in $20,000 over a ten-year period. If you waited to save, you end up putting in $70,000 over thirty-five years.

Not only that, if you had just kept saving $2,000 per year from when you were 25 until you turned 70 (earning that same 8%), you would have $883,000, which is more than double if you started at 35.

Give your money a raise. Get started today.

CHAPTER 13

Would You Lend You Money?

Sometimes the best way to learn something is by just asking yourself a simple question or two. Be honest with your answers. More sophisticated folks may say you should be self-reflective. For a simple money guy like me, it seems easier to just ask yourself some questions.

Here goes. Would you lend yourself money? Ask yourself, "Would I lend me money?" If this feels funny, don't ask yourself out loud. The real trick to learning from the question is being honest about your answer.

So would you lend you money? Before you answer, consider a few factors:

1. Have you borrowed and repaid money (from anyone) before?

2. Do you keep your commitments to others?

3. Do you pay your bills on time?

4. Do you take care of the things you own?

5. Does your credit card have a big balance owed on it?

6. Have you had a steady job for more than 1 year?

If your answers to those questions are:

1. No

2. Not always

3. Most of them

4. Sort of

5. Yes

6. No

Why would you take the risk of lending yourself money? You don't have a track record of promptly repaying loans. You don't keep commitments. You already owe a lot of money on a credit card that you are not paying off.

Ah, but this time you tell yourself, "I'll be different. I promise I will repay me. I'm going to change starting now."

The fact is, your history says a lot more about you than what you say you are going to do. That is how the rest of the world is going to evaluate lending you money. It's the way you (I) should evaluate you (me).

Ghandi said, "Action expresses priorities."

Maybe a simpler way to make this point is to repeat one of my dad's favorite sayings, "I'd rather owe you money than cheat you out of it." Of course he was kidding. Dad paid his debts, which is one reason I learned early on to pay mine. If you don't pay your debts to others you are cheating them out of it.

Let's go through the questions again (positively):

1. Have you borrowed and repaid money (from anyone) before?

2. Do you keep your commitments to others?

3. Do you pay your bills on time?

4. Do you take care of the things you own?

5. Does your credit card have a big balance owed on it?

6. Have you had a steady job for more than 1 year?

Positive answers:

1. Yes

2. I don't make commitments I can't keep.

3. Always

4. Yes

5. Nope, $0 balance, pay it off every month.

6. Yup, been at the same place 3 years now.

If these are your answers, why wouldn't you take the risk of lending yourself money? You're responsible, you pay your debts, you hold a steady job, you keep commitments. Again, your history proves you are going to keep your promise to repay yourself.

Your actions (paying money back on time) express your priorities (honoring your commitments).

You are not a big risk . . . to yourself or to others.

This is what you want lenders to think of you: "Geez, look at the history of this person being responsible. They work, they pay, they don't owe lots of money to others. They are downright boring."

Be boring.

So, a place to start understanding money is by honestly looking at yourself and asking if you have been a good user of money. If not, you need to be. If you are, you'll be a sought after customer of banks. That's a good place to be. This book is going to help you get to that good place.

CHAPTER 14

How Do Banks Think?

Why should you care?

How do banks think? Really? Who cares? You thought we were talking about money . . . your money. You may believe that what banks think is not important to you. You may think that only bankers need to know how banks think. You are entitled to your opinion.

But it will cost you.

Think about this: banks think about and handle money . . . a lot. Even a bank robber, a bank's archenemy, goes to banks because that is where the money is. Knowing what banks think is very valuable.

The hard truth is that it does matter to you. Unless you are fabulously, independently wealthy, how banks think will matter to you at many key points in your lifetime. And even if you are fabulously wealthy, understanding how money works, and how banks work, will help to keep you that way. Stay fabulous.

Perspective and empathy are two of the most important keys to your financial future. Empathy? For banks? Am I nuts?

Do not confuse empathy with sympathy. Empathy is being able to understand someone else's feelings. This will help you throughout your life. Believe it or not, bankers are people, too. If you can understand them, you will be better off. Simply put - you want to know about money. Bankers know about money. Why not learn from them and take what they're giving? Why not know what they know?

It is always valuable to understand how someone else, whether it is a banker, partner, significant other or insignificant other, looks at a situation. If you can understand someone else's point of view, it will always work in your favor.

At some point, you will likely want or need to borrow money for something: home, car, boat, education, etc. You can borrow money for almost anything except retirement.

When you want to borrow money, it will serve you well to understand how the lender will evaluate you as a potential borrower. What will make it easier for you to obtain the loan? Lenders and borrowers call this process "getting approved."

Before we explain how a bank thinks, let's first look at how most of us think about money and income. Remember, from the time we were children, the people who taught us that money has value (parents, aunts, uncles and other adults), also cautioned us with, "Don't let anybody know how much money you have."

Then, once we began to earn money by working, they would tell us, "It's nobody else's business how much money you make."

Fast forward – you are now a young adult. You need a place to safely store your money. Where? Most people don't literally earn a paper paycheck any longer. Employers provide them with an electronic pay stub and deposit the money into an account at some type of financial institution or a card with your pay loaded on it. It still is typically tied to an account at a bank.

So you arrive at the bank beaming with pride while guarding your privacy. You request to open an account to hold your money. After all, who wouldn't want your money? You say, "I would like to open an account please." The first questions from the banker go against the grain of everything you've been taught about keeping your money to yourself, starting with "How much money do you have?"

Boom. Internal alarms go off in your head. You remember the advice that the people you know, love and trust have been giving you all your life. "Don't tell anybody how much money you have or how much you make."

Who does this banker think he or she is to pry open the lid into your private money world? More invasive questions follow, including:

· How much money do you have to open the account?

· How much money will you be adding to it?

· How often will you be taking money out of the account?

· How will you be taking the money out?

· In what amounts?

Reluctantly, you answer the banker's questions, but probably not before you ask them why they need to know that information.

Well, why do they need to know?

The first answer is simple. The bank wants you to get the account that best suits you. It is not good for you to have an account that does not provide the services and access to your money when and how you need it. It's not good for the bank, either. And, you do not want to overpay for services you do not need or will not be using.

The second answer is also simple, but is rarely seen or understood. The government requires banks to know their customers, their identity, their business, their source of income, where they live, and more. It is driven by literally thousands of pages of law and regulation, most of it coming from the federal government.

Everyone should want the banks doing this. It really helps protect your money (and everyone else's) and helps the government identify, follow, and catch the bad guys. Banks have to report a lot of information about their customers and about themselves to the government because the government requires it.

Depositing your money is relatively easy. Let's look at the other side of money… borrowing. You need to borrow some. Now the questions become even more invasive.

· Where do you work?

· For how long?

· Where do you live?

· For how long?

· Have you borrowed money before?

· How much money do you make?

· What is your budget for living expenses?

· Do you have a credit card?

· What is the balance?

· What assets do you own?

· What are they worth?

· Would you provide us with your income tax returns for the last two years?

· Could you fill out a personal financial statement?

· What is the purpose of the loan?

· What is the total purchase price?

· How much is your down payment?

You start asking yourself your own questions:

- Why do banks ask so many private financial questions?
- Who do they think they are?
- Do you really have to give them all this information?

Banks have to ask these questions. You only need to answer them if you want to borrow money.

Another point - the government expects the bank to ask these questions. They expect the bank to determine if you qualify for and can repay the loan. They examine every bank regularly to ensure that the bank is operating soundly, which includes making loans to borrowers that have the ability to repay them.

It's not all bad. This helps make banks safe.

Truth be told, it is not all that different from the way you would approach lending money to someone. When it's your money that is being borrowed, you will realize that you would want to know the same things that a bank wants to know.

Comedian Bob Hope once famously said, "A bank will lend you money, if you can prove you do not need it." Bob was a legendary comedian but he was not exactly accurate. Here is a better way to look at it - banks will lend you money if you can prove you can repay it.

Let's look at a simple example. If you are with a friend who has forgotten their wallet and you are out for lunch, you would likely lend them $10. Unless it's that friend that never pays anyone back (we all have this friend for some reason), you feel fully confident they would repay you once they had their wallet. Why? It is a relatively small amount of money. And it's your friend.

If that same friend forgot their wallet and was buying a $500 watch, you would be a little more reluctant to lend the money because a) it's a lot more money, and b) you are not so sure they can afford that watch. So, you would likely make a judgment the same way a bank would: do you think your friend is capable of repaying the money? You do think like a bank after all. Who would have thought that? The Banking Paradox – Banks are lenders not investors.

A key to understanding how banks think is to first understand the difference between an investor and a lender. Basically, banks are not investors or owners. Let's not get too deep into investing (types of investments, who can be an investor, where you can make investments, and more). That's another book. Actually, it would be countless other books. Either way, let's keep moving.

We just want to understand why a bank is not an investor or an owner. Banks are a nearly unlimited source of money and a very limited source of money at the same time. How can that be? What happened to simple?

Well, let's first look at what banks do not do. Banks don't make money by buying and selling properties or businesses. They do not want to take on another person's risks. There are other organizations and people that do that. They are called investors.

Very briefly, let's think about business investors and owners being the same thing. It will help you understand your role. Investors are owners of a company or business, they are not lenders.

Why do we call investors owners? When they invest their money, it is not a loan. Investors don't expect to simply be paid a rate of interest for the use of their money. They are actually buying a piece (large, small, or even all) of a business.

They want to share in the success of the business. How? By having the value of their investment rise as the business grows, or receiving a share of the profits. They also watch the value of their investment fall as the business shrinks. They share in the losses. As owners, they are accepting the risks of the business. After all, they own it.

By contrast, a bank is not an owner. Why not? They are not buying a piece of a business. When they make a loan, they are providing the use of money (loan) to the owner in return for a fee (interest). They expect to be paid the fee (interest) every month, on top of repayment of a small portion of the loan (principal). Ultimately, banks expect to be repaid the entire amount of the loan (principal) plus the agreed upon interest. This is no different than our earlier example of how you got your dollar paid back from Wimpy . . . I mean your buddy. In that case, you were repaid $1.10 - $1 of principal and .10 of interest.

As individuals, we borrow money for homes, cars, vacations, boats, education and more. As the individual, you are the investor, or the owner. Now we can argue whether the things you borrow money for as an individual are truly investments which we expect to go up in value. In fact most are not, and don't go up in value. As individuals, we are really buyers/owners, and most things we buy fall in value. We know that before we buy them. Cars, furniture and boats don't go up in value as they get older and used. They go down in value. Yet we still like to own the stuff.

The difference between investors and owners is that they own things for different reasons. Investors expect to make money. Owners want to use and/or enjoy something. One exception to this can be a house. I say *can be* because homes don't always go up in value, but if a home is properly maintained and is located in a desirable area, they generally will hold value or grow in value.

By contrast if you borrowed money to go on vacation, once it is over, there is zero value left besides the personal experience you get for it (priceless). The vacation and your memories can be emotionally priceless, but you cannot sell your vacation or experiences to anyone else. And please don't bore them with a zillion pictures, either.

When you buy something because you were able to secure a loan from a bank or other lender, that lender expects you to repay the loan based exactly on terms of the loan agreement. You will make X payments at $X amount at X% interest. It is all very specific and clearly defined and explained. If it is not, run away from that lender and the loan!

Let's stick with borrowing money for the home as an example. It's likely you agreed to a long-term, fixed-rate loan (which is commonly called a mortgage). Something like 360 monthly payments of $1,000 per month at 5% interest. Once the 360 monthly payments are made, you own the home 'free and clear' and the bank is no longer involved. Prior to that, you were still the owner... you were always the owner. The bank as the lender simply had a legal right to take it, if you did not repay their loan.

Why can they take it? Because you signed a document that said you would repay a loan to them based on the value the house, and if you don't, you allow them the right to take the house. You can give it to them voluntarily, or they can force you to do so via a process called foreclosure.

In fact, if you want to pay off the loan earlier, you can do so, typically without any penalties or additional costs. When the payments are made on time or the loan is paid off early, both the homeowner and the lender are happy.

In this case, you are the investor (or owner). You are buying the home. You will own it, all of it. The bank is the lender. They provide you with the funds to purchase the home on the basis that that you agreed to pay them back. They expect to be paid a fee (interest) every month, on top of repayment of a small portion of the loan (principal). Ultimately, they expect to be repaid the entire amount of the loan (principal) plus the agreed upon interest. If you sell the home, regardless of whether you make or lose money on the sale, the bank wants to be repaid its loan in full.

If you make money on the home, will you share it with the bank? Not likely. Therefore, if you lose money on the home, why would you expect the bank to share in your loss? Remember, you are the investor . . . the owner. You accepted that risk. The bank is the lender.

Why would you borrow money to buy a home? Simple, it would take nearly forever to save enough money to buy a home with cash. If it took you 30 years to save enough money to pay cash for a home, where would you live during that time? Through the magic of banking, you are able to buy the home by borrowing the money today, and agreeing to pay for it over 30 years.

Why do that? You will derive more value by living in the home for the next 30 years rather than waiting 30 years to buy it. You are willing to pay the necessary interest rate to enjoy the home today. In addition, you hope it will increase in value over that time.

Problems happen when payments do not happen. When the borrower (in this case, you) fails to make the payments, you are failing to keep the promise.

Banks have owners just like other businesses do. The owners of a bank are tied to its success. If the bank fails, the owners lose everything invested. If the bank succeeds, they share in its profits and increased value.

What business risks does a bank take? Once we understand that, we will understand how they think. A bank's business is to take in deposits and to make loans. They can't overpay for deposits (too high a rate) or their costs of running the business will be too high. They can't undercharge for loans (charge too little interest rate) or they won't cover all the costs of doing business.

Remember, money makes money and money costs money. Banks regularly experience both.

They must manage their cost of deposits (deposit rates) vs. the loan pricing (loan rates). This is called the Net Interest Margin (NIM). If the bank pays 1% for deposits, and charges 4% for loans, it has a NIM of 3%. If it pays 3.5% for deposits and charges 7.5% for loans, it has a NIM of 4%.

From that difference in interest rates, the bank must cover its operating costs – employee salaries and benefits, marketing, technology, rent, insurances, travel, education, furniture, charitable contributions and more. It's not easy; in fact it is far more complex than I am explaining here.

That is how banks make money - pay less for deposits and charge more for loans. The bigger risk banks face lies in choosing to whom they lend money. Banks don't want your business, car, house, or anything else for which you borrowed money. They want you to repay the loan as planned.

The bank's key business risk is in selecting borrowers that will successfully repay their loans. If they were perfect at this, they would have no business risk and they would be repaid in full and on time on every loan. Banks are not perfect at selecting borrowers. Nobody is perfect.

There are too many factors that they cannot control that make this impossible. Businesses fail, buildings burn, people lose jobs, partners argue, people steal, people get sick, couples divorce, families fracture, employees quit, property values fall, competitors get stronger, tenants move out, people die . . . and on and on.

Despite all these uncontrollable factors, banks still attempt to be perfect on selecting only those borrowers that will repay their loans. How accurate do the banks have to be? Do the banks have to be right on the money?

On the average, banks need to be right 99% of the time to be successful long term. That is their business risk; determining if you are a credit-worthy borrower and if they should risk lending you money. Do they believe that you will repay your loan regardless of the circumstances you encounter?

With all these bad things potentially happening, how are banks able to make decisions about to whom they will lend money with such a high degree of accuracy?

Banks take additional steps to recover their loan if you cannot make the payments.

Wouldn't you do the same? If your friend asks to you to loan them $25,000, would you do it? Wouldn't you want to know that they can repay the loan? If they could not repay the loan, how could you get your $25,000 back? Would you be happy your friend had a new car and you had lost the $25,000 you loaned them? Of course not.

When you think of lending money like this, banks almost seem human. Almost.

Now, let's look at how banks attempt to protect themselves. They minimize risk. Here's how: First, banks will look at how much money you make, or your income.

Then they will look at what your monthly payments or obligations are, which generally include:

·Mortgage or rent

·Minimum credit card payments

·Car loan

·Student loans

·Alimony/child support payments

·Other loans

This is the total amount you spend each month on debt. Let's say you make $6,000 in gross pay per month. If you have $0 in debt payments, you have a 0% debt-to-income ratio (DTI); how much debt you have to pay per month vs. how much money you make per month. If you have a car payment ($500) and a house payment ($1,400) and minimum credit card payment ($100) your debt payments total $2,000, you have a 33% DTI ($2,000/$6,000).

There are guidelines that lenders use in determining an acceptable DTI. Generally it should not be above 43% (with $6,000 monthly income this would not be more than $2,580). Essentially, they are making sure you can afford to make the house payment each month and that you can afford all your other payments and have something left for living expenses. That is their first level of protection.

Next, banks look at the value of what you are purchasing. Whether it is a home, car, computer, RV, factory, or anything else, they are going to lend you less than the total purchase price or value. If the purchase price is $100,000; they will lend you 75% - 80%; about $75,000 to $80,000. You have to fund the rest. That's the down payment.

So, if you buy a $100,000 house, make a $20,000 down payment, you need an $80,000 loan, which equals 80% of the house value which means the loan value compared to the house value is 80% ($80,000/$100,000) or a loan-to-value of 80%.

Why do banks lend you less than the house value? Well, once

again, the answer is protection. If you cannot make the payments and they have to take back and resell what you bought, they will never get the price you paid for it, especially after all the expenses they will incur (sale commissions, repairs, back taxes, maintenance, insuring it while owning it, etc.)

Also, the bank's general feeling is if you have money invested into something, you are less likely to want to lose it; therefore you will work harder to make payments and keep it. The old saying is to have some 'skin in the game'. Your skin in this game is a down payment.

What is collateral? The asset or thing you are buying becomes the collateral for the loan. Banks will also hold a legal interest in the asset you purchase. That means they can take ownership of the asset should you not make payments. Why do they do this? To protect themselves against loss should you stop making payments. Even if they don't recover the entire amount of the loan by reselling the collateral (what you bought), banks will at least minimize their losses by recovering as much as they can from the sale.

There are further measures that banks can take to minimize their risk of loss if you do not repay them, but I think you can see if your business fails, you lose your income, you die, or stop making payments, the bank will not lose its entire loan. Nor should it. The bank is not the owner . . . it is a lender.

So now who cares what a bank thinks? If you ever need money, you do.

CHAPTER 15

The All You Can Borrow Buffet a.k.a.
"What Loan for What Purpose?"

When it comes to borrowing money, it can be very confusing to find the right loan for what you need. Why? There are so many different offerings from so many different lenders. It's almost like lenders are saying, "Come on in to the 'All-You-Can-Borrow-Buffet.' You can choose from dozens of different loans or dishes. Load up. Have all you want. After all, it's all you can borrow. When you find something you really like, you can go back for more. Borrow up."

If you don't believe me, google the term "loans" and see how many entries come up. I got over 25 million entries in less than half a second. Page through a Sunday newspaper and you will see several loan offers. Listen to the radio in your car (or really anywhere) and you will hear even more offers. Watch TV and more lenders are making offers to you.

They are everywhere. What are they offering? Car loans, home equity lines of credit, home mortgages, debt consolidation loans, and more. Of course, each one promises the lowest cost and the lowest rate. How can that be? The answer is very simple. It can't be . . . and it isn't.

Now what are you supposed to do? Take a deep breath and think about why you need a loan. What makes the most sense and works best for you? I know, you are thinking, "You don't get it, Joe. I don't know what is best for me."

That is the whole point. I do get it. I'll help you think through that in just a minute, which is easier than it first appears. Once you have a good idea of what it is that you want, find a reputable lender . . . one you can trust to help guide you.

What do you want? Really, it's not a loan. What you want is what you need the loan for. The loan is one way for you to get it. What you really want is a car, a home, a boat, or something else that's of value to you. And you want to own it.

Think about the value of what that is. How long will what you want hold its value? This is the challenge. When you first buy something, it's all shiny and new. As the great philosopher Flounder said in *Animal House,* "Oh boy, is this great?!?"

Then reality, and depreciation, set in. Depreciation simply means dropping in value, usually due to wear and tear. Cars don't last all that long. New cars drop in value over the years just like used cars. Depending on the car, it has some decent value over a three to seven year period.

Bonus Rule #1 in Borrowing for Cars - Don't borrow for more years than the car will have value. In fact, borrow for *fewer* years than it will have value.

Thankfully, homes are a bit of a different story. They can increase, decrease or stay at a fairly steady value. If you maintain your home and it's located in a decent area, it's more likely to go up than down in value over time. Homes should have value for many years, so you can borrow for them over a longer period.

Since the 2008 financial crash, a home's rising value is no longer a slam dunk, as so many people found out so painfully. A home can still be a good investment. You really have to do your homework to buy one that is a good investment. Let's get back to loans.

How do you find a reputable lender? Start with a bank. Why? First of all, banks want to be an important business to the communities they serve. They want to be viewed as reputable, respected businesses and leaders in their communities. They want people to refer friends, family and business associates to them. They want to serve families from generation to generation. The only way to do that is to consistently provide solid financial advice and services to people and other businesses in the community.

Second of all, banks are highly regulated by state and federal regulators. They undergo regular examinations by those regulators. What does that mean for you? You can be confident of dealing with a bank. Regulators ensure that banks:

- are practicing safe and sound financial practices
- do not practice unfair and deceptive advertising
- do not discriminate in lending to certain groups of people

These are just a few. Believe me, there's more . . . a lot more.

Look for knowledgeable, experienced lenders at reputable banks that can provide you with good advice on your lending need.

Speaking of your need, is it a line of credit, a term loan, second mortgage, mortgage, revolving loan, auto loan, home equity line of credit (HELOC, pronounced 'he-lock') that you need? Do you really care what the loan is called? Heck no. What you care about is getting the loan you need to get what you want. You need someone that deals with that stuff every day. Someone who can explain it to you, help you through the process, and give you good advice. You find those people at banks.

Now let's return to the 'all-you-can-borrow-buffet' for just a minute. At any buffet, it is easy to make mistakes; choosing something that tastes bad, choosing something that looks delicious, but tastes bad, choosing something you just do not like, taking too much of something, taking something you think is chicken, but turns out to be fish or simply failing to take something that's really good because you did not see it.

When it comes to borrowing, all those same things can happen. You can borrow too much, you can agree to the wrong terms, you can overpay on interest, you can miss out on a great rate, you can take a loan you no longer like but are stuck with, you can have a loan you thought had a fixed rate, but it changes (looks good but tastes bad).

Is it possible to avoid these mistakes? Of course it is. In order to do so, you've got to find experienced people you can trust who will give you good advice today and in the future. Lending money is complicated and individualized. Over time, you will buy houses, cars, and more.

Your financial needs change throughout your life. Certain loan products can give you really easy access to borrowing money with a phone call, electronic entry, or writing a check. Still, everyone is borrowing a different amount for a different reason. Everyone has a different ability to repay. Let's sort this all out.

First, let's go back to why you need to borrow money. Is it a car, a house, a vacation, boat, education, furniture? That is your call.

Now, for how long should you borrow the money? The easy answer is for as short a period of time as possible that you can afford. But how do you select a loan that matches your need, your ability to pay, for the right length of time, and at a proper rate?

Let's start with a car. You are buying your first car. With taxes, title, license, purchase price, dealer fees and everything else added in, you are paying $13,000 for the car. It's a used car and it's in good shape. You figure it will easily last you 3 years, probably up to 5 years, but that may be stretching it a bit. You have been a good saver and you have $3,000 for a down payment. You will finance $10,000. So, if you could borrow money at the following rates, for the following time periods, here is what your payments will be:

Length of Loan	3 Years	4 Years	5 Years
Number of Payments	36	48	60
Monthly Payment (0% interest rate)	$277.77	$208.33	$166.66

Zero interest (0%) is only likely in certain situations (usually only for new cars and usually from the manufacturer). The point here is how the amount of the monthly payment can help you make a good loan choice. Next, you'll also get an idea of how interest adds to the cost.

Let's say you think the car has value for three years. If in three years, you finish making payments, you own the car free and clear from any loans. It is still worth something, and you say you can easily make a payment of $277.77. Select the 36 month term. Let's say you cannot swing $277.77 per month. If the most you figure you can afford is $210, well, it looks like the 48 month loan fits well for a payment and within the time period you feel comfortable that the car will last. That is a good decision.

What if you could afford $250 per month but you decide you only want to pay $166.66 over a five-year period so you have more spending money? Remember, you don't think the car is likely to last that long. If it does last only 4 years, you will still make payments for another year, after it no longer has any value. That is not a good decision.

If you choose the 3 year term, you would be payment free for a year before the car died. If you chose the 4 year term, you matched up pretty well.

Since you are not likely to get a 0% loan, let's see how the interest rate enters the picture. What does the interest really cost? Generally speaking, the longer the term you borrow money, the higher the interest rate. Sometimes there are specials or other things that impact this, but you should know that in general, the longer time you borrow money for, the higher the rate.

Length of Loan	3 Years	4 Years	5 Years
Number of Payments	36	48	60
Monthly Payment (5% interest rate)	$299.71	$230.99	N/A
Monthly Payment (10% interest rate)	$322.67	$253.63	$212.47

Notice how in the example above you cannot borrow money for 60 months at 5%. Why not? They're not going to give it to you for the same price as a shorter loan. You can only get a loan for that long at a higher rate, in this case 10%.

Also notice that you can pay 5% or 10% interest for the same loan length. Why? Different lenders may charge different rates. Compare the rates and choose the lower one (assuming they are not charging any other fees for the lower rate).

The same ideas apply here – what can you afford for a monthly payment, and how long will the car last? You can see the difference in payments with the cost of interest added.

First question – what can you afford? Remember, *borrow for as short of a period of time that you can afford.* You said that you could afford the $250, so 48 month option works fine. How long will the car last? You figured 48 months. That works. Done.

Why not stretch to 60 months to lower your payment? You pay more for the money (higher interest rate of 10%) and you pay more because you are paying to use the money for a longer period of time (60 months vs. 48 months), which costs you more.

Does it ever make sense to borrow money for a longer period of time and pay a higher rate of interest?

Yes, it can make sense.

Let's use the example of a home to make the point. Remember, when you borrow money for a home, the loan is commonly referred to as a mortgage. When you borrow money for a home, you will have several options. Let's pretend there are just two, which are the most common.

You can borrow money for 15 years or for 30 years. In both cases, you will pay a fee for the use of the money. That fee, or your cost, is called interest, which is used in determining your payment.

In both cases you will make a monthly payment. You make those monthly payments for the duration of the loan – 15 years or 30 years.

Remember, we said you pay a higher interest rate (it costs you more) to borrow for a longer time than a shorter time. Here are the rates and the monthly payment for a $100,000 home loan at the time I am writing this:

15 years @ 3.00% = $690.58/month

30 years @ 4.00% = $477.72/month

A $100,000 home mortgage will have payments of $690.58 for 15 years or $477.72 for 30 years.

Again, we are keeping it simple. For our purposes, you don't need to know how the payments were calculated. But, you can clearly see that you would pay more per month for the 15-year mortgage than you would for the 30-year mortgage.

Why? Because you are making payments over a much shorter period of time. This is true even though the rate is lower. If you can comfortably afford $690.58 per month for your mortgage, this could be a good choice.

Let's look at it differently for a minute. Your payment on the 30-year mortgage is just $477.72 per month. If you chose this option, your payments are even more comfortable for you. Maybe this choice even allows you to save some money for your kids' college education or for that car.

You know you can make the 15-year monthly payment, but it might make things tight. It's okay to pay for it over a longer period of time. What if you select the 30-year and its lower monthly payments, feeling more confident you can make the payments? Then you might be able to pay more per month than the payment, or that once you save some money and you don't need to use it for another specific purpose you can use it to pay down on the mortgage.

What you've done is lock in guaranteed fixed rate financing at a low 4% for 30 years. Can you predict what financial issues you will have to deal with over the next 30 years? That's not likely, but for an extra cost of 1% (remember, the 15 year is 3%), you've given yourself lots of flexibility and choices.

Flexibility and choices are good.

Will it cost you more to make payments for 30 years instead of 15? Of course it will, and here is the math: just multiply the payment amount by the number of payments:

$477.72 x 360 = $171,979.20 (30 year)

$690.58 x 180 = $124,304.40 (15 year)

$47,674.80

The difference is $47,674.80. That is a lot of money, but remember, we are talking about that over a 15 to 30 year period. And remember, your payments were $212.96 less per month. That pays a lot of other monthly bills.

In that time, life changes, incomes change, expenses change. And, if you pay the loan off in say 12 to 16 years through extra payments, the difference in cost is much less. That is important. These are not minor differences in fees or rates. They matter. If you have a banker you can trust, they will do the math for you and explain finance to you so you can understand it.

If they can't do the math for you, find a different banker. We are only focused on the rate you are paying to use money. We are assuming fees are the same. Be sure they are. If your lender cannot explain why their fees are different and how you benefit – find a different lender.

A final important point needs to be made here. I just outlined how to select a loan based on length of time you are borrowing, how long you expect what you are buying will last, and the interest rate. These are just a few factors that will help you make good selections.

Finally (this time I mean it), I ignored how payments are made up of principal and interest to keep things simple. Here's a bonus lesson: Loans are repaid based on an amortization schedule. If this sounds complicated, that's because it kind of is.

The simple thing to know is that while your payment stays the same each month, the amount that goes toward your principal and your interest changes. It's all defined in an amortization table. What is that? It's just a listing of the planned payments and the amount of each payment that goes to principal and interest.

The simple rule to know here is this: *more of your payment goes to interest early in the payments and less goes to interest in your payment later.*

It's just the opposite for principal: *less is paid early and more is paid later.*

Your key takeaways from this chapter:

1. Know the length of the loan you should get.
2. The lower the rate, the less it costs you (Again, assuming the same fees).

CHAPTER 16

What's the Credit Score?

Who's winning the borrowing game? This is a great question. You won't know until you know the score. How can you tell? Let's look at your score – your credit score.

What is a credit score? It is a number. A calculation that tells a lender how likely you are to repay them, based on how you've performed at paying lenders in your past. The higher your score, the more likely you are to repay; the lower, the less likely.

Next, why is it important to have a good credit score? Your credit score impacts how much money it costs you to use someone else's money. Remember, you are paying interest to use someone else's money. This will be true for credit cards, cars, homes, and for anything else for which you borrow money.

Plan on it always costing you more when you use someone else's money if you are not a good borrower with a good credit score.

How will you know? Read the fine print in any advertisement for money (known as disclosures). It will tell you that you need to qualify for the advertised rate.

Will they still lend you money if you don't qualify? Maybe not, if you are a bad risk. If you are an "okay" risk, they will simply charge you more to use their money (more interest). The higher the risk, the higher the price.

When it comes to your credit score, a higher score is always better. A lower score is always worse. If you are familiar with the concept of something being on sale, think of the cost of borrowing money this way:

Money is always on sale for people with high credit scores. That is kind of a big deal. It means they pay lower interest rates.

A high credit score can save you money in other ways. They are even becoming a measure of how responsible you are. Many insurance companies charge less for insurance when you have a high credit score. That also means your credit score might be as good as or better than your driving record as an indicator of how responsible of a driver you are.

Plan on employers checking your credit score as part of a background check. If you have a low credit score, you might not score the job. Ouch. Not getting paid is worse than not getting credit.

You don't need to know how the number is calculated. It is actually very complicated and done by computer using several mathematical algorithms. Heck, you don't even need to know what an algorithm is.

What you do need to know is what positively and negatively impacts your score. It is this simple:

1. Pay your bills on time.

Pay all of your bills (rent, utilities, phone, TV, medical, loans, etc.). This is really important. Pay your bills on or before the due date.

2. Borrow less money than you can.

What? If your credit card can have a balance of $1,000, never let the balance get that high. If your home equity loan can be up to $50,000, never let it get that high. Just because you can borrow money does not mean you need to borrow it. Showing lenders that you don't borrow money just because you can shows you are very responsible.

3. How long have you been using credit (credit history)?

It's good to have a credit card, even though you don't need to use it. Use it once in a while to show you will repay the borrowed amount quickly. Again you are showing them over time you don't borrow money just because you can. If you have a mortgage on a home and regularly make your payment on time, that is a good thing. Making payments on student loans and all loans regularly and timely is a good thing.

4. Don't open a credit account every time someone asks you.

Those credit card offers are tempting, but opening a lot of credit card accounts negatively impacts your credit score. Opening lots of new credit accounts in a short period of time sends a message that you are not likely a responsible user of credit. So, don't open accounts at Kohl's, Boston Store, Target, and Home Depot all in one month. It's okay to have multiple accounts (even though you don't likely need them all), just don't open them all at the same time. The same rules apply to the limits on multiple cards. Don't have balances on all of them at your limit.

There's more, but your credit score really comes down to this: if you pay on time, establish a history of doing so, don't open too many credit accounts at one time, and don't actually borrow the maximum from each lender, you will have a good credit score. Most importantly, focus on paying on time and not being maxed out on borrowing.

You'll have the highest credit score and you'll be winning the game. No question about it.

CHAPTER 17

How to be a Desirable Borrower . . . to a Bank.

When it is time for you to borrow money, you want to be a desirable borrower . . . a person a bank wants to lend money to.

Why? Better service, better rates, more choices. If you can impress a bank by showing that you are responsible, reliable, organized and honest, they will all want to lend money to you. You will have choices. Choices are good.

If you talk to more than one banker, how do you choose the best one for you? Easy, do business with someone you like and trust. Life's too short to deal with someone you don't trust or like. Find someone who provides you with the best rate and terms. If the banker with the better rate is a jerk, tell the other one you like he needs to meet or beat the jerk's rate and terms. Most often, they will. Or find another one that will.

Now that you have the loan, you want the bank to treat you well. They will if you keep your financial commitments to them and others. Then, if you don't like their service, you can go to another bank that provides better service.

Once again, making timely payments = freedom. I know that because I see it happen all the time. People often switch to my bank because they don't feel they are being treated well by their bank. Banks don't want to lose a desirable customer to another bank for any reason, least of all bad service.

When you walk into the bank, look good. Don't show up in torn jeans and a t-shirt. You can do that later when you've made lots of money and proved you are a great client. If you are older, you'll be eccentric. Right now, you want to be desirable. You want them to want you. Appearing professional helps. If you don't like them, you can tell them no. You don't have to wear a suit. Just don't show up in dirty jeans and a t-shirt.

Next, bring some information with you that the bank is going to want. This will show that you are organized, and that you know what you have, what you owe, and what you make.

Here's what to bring:

- Your last 2 to 4 pay statements
- Your tax returns for the past 2 years
- A listing of what you own and owe (a personal financial statement)
- A list of debts: credit card, mortgage, car, student . . . (balance and monthly payment)
- Monthly obligations: rent, gas, electric, telephone . . .
- Work history
- Length of time at your current address

It's pretty simple. You'll be organized . . . and desirable.

CHAPTER 18

How Do You Keep the Passion?

Now that you've made yourself desirable to your bank, how do you keep the flame alive? Easy, do the things you are supposed to do, like make your payments on time, and don't overdraw your account. That could be the end of this chapter, but I'd like to prove my point here by telling you a couple of the things bankers keep track of. This will also help you understand how banks think:

1. Overdrafts

When you spend more money than you have in your account (usually your checking account), that's called an overdraft, or overdrawing your account. To a banker, this is very bad. You are spending money you don't have. It's a red flag that you could become a big problem.

Banks track them daily and report them on a monthly basis to their board. Here's what a report looks like:

Current Overdrafts

Account Number	Account Name	Full Date	Account Ledger Balance	Account Ctd Times
		08/31/2012	-53.72	18
		08/31/2012	-58,353.68	23
		08/31/2012	-7,840.01	6
		08/31/2012	-607.86	2
		08/31/2012	-1,514.16	1
		08/31/2012	-7.68	5
		08/31/2012	-104.58	10
		08/31/2012	-9.98	1

Consecutive Overdrafts

Account Number	Account Name	Full Date	Account Consecutive Days Overdrawn	Account Ledger Balance	Account Ctd Times Overdrawn
		08/31/2012	7	-53.72	18
		08/31/2012	92	-58,353.68	23
		08/31/2012	4	-7,840.01	6
		08/31/2012	4	-607.86	2
		08/31/2012	4	-1,514.16	1
		08/31/2012	4	-7.68	5
		08/31/2012	5	-104.58	10
		08/31/2012	4	-9.98	1

Don't make your payments late.

Banks track this as closely as overdrafts. Late payments are also reported to the board. Here's how that report looks:

Past due Loans -30 Days +
Data As Of: August 31, 2012

Name	Account Number	Ledger Balance	Amount Past Due	Interest Past Due	Number of Days Past Due
		538,604.92	538,604.92	38,639.61	1020
		307,322.49	307,322.49	36,873.40	600
		613,572.71	613,572.71	47,288.94	555
		99,815.01	99,815.01	5,534.07	510
		712,069.03	712,069.03	24,089.56	300
		9,832.26	9,832.26	5,155.58	270
		22,055.14	22,055.14	942.83	240
		222,868.09	222,868.09	4,258.74	210
		74,463.84	74,463.84	2,755.80	196
		79,038.05	79,038.05	2,619.97	180
		41,979.56	41,979.56	0.00	166
		553,155.56	553,155.56	8,255.06	120
		773,423.34	773,423.34	9,835.94	90
		47,410.19	1,072.59	1,072.59	76
		93,896.41	881.24	881.24	60
		69,043.35	760.62	760.62	60

Your name showing up on these reports is a problem, especially if it happens with any frequency. Actually, it's an indication that you have a problem that could become the bank's problem. Bankers don't like problems, especially other people's problems.

Now imagine that your name has been on either of these lists a few times and your loan needs to be renewed, or you want to borrow more money, or increase your credit card limit. What do you think their response should be? What do you think it will be?

Likely, they won't want to lend you more money. Why would they if you are struggling to make payments now?

Imagine this conversation at the bank about you:

"Joe wants to borrow more money for a new car. This is the same guy who's been late with payments 3 times in the past and overdrafted his account twice in the last year. I don't think we should lend him more money."

Do bankers meet and talk like that? You bet they do. They also talk about their customers who are responsible:

"He's made every payment on time, paid down early on the principal, and he always has money in his account. He's the type of person we want to lend money to. You bet he can borrow more."

Passion is in the eye of the beholder. Keep the passion in your banking relationship by making payments on time and keeping a positive balance in your account. That's passion made easy.

CHAPTER 19

What is House Poor?

Being poor is no fun. Sure, some people say it builds character and money cannot buy happiness. The people who say this usually have lots of money. Worrying about not having enough to pay your bills every month is simply no fun. It certainly won't bring you happiness.

Poorness does not equal happiness. It equals stress.

Making good money (you define "good") and still feeling like you don't have any because your money all goes to make payments each month is not a lot of laughs, either. You make lots of money, but you have nothing left to spend or to save. How did you get here?

There's an old saying that goes like this . . . "You don't want to be house poor." What does that mean? It's simple. You spent more on a house than you should have. How do we know that? Too much of your income goes toward making the house payment.

If your income each month after all taxes and deductions is $3,000, and your house payment including property taxes is $2,700, that is way too much of your income to spend on housing. That leaves you $300 for food, gas, car, clothing, insurance, TV, internet, utilities, and any other payments you must make. At the end of the month, you don't have anything left for fun: vacations, dining out, entertainment, donations or anything else. You are house poor.

If your payment were only $1,000 per month, you would have $2,000 per month for everything else. That should leave you enough money to make all your other payments, and have some to spend on fun and to save.

Banks can help you understand the amount of money you should commit to a monthly house payment. Listen to them. They know this stuff. Their numbers work.

Don't get talked into a more expensive home than you can afford (or should afford) because someone else thinks you should or because they will earn a commission on it. What you can afford vs. what you want to afford applies to homes as much as it does to cars or anything else.

You can have a rich home life if you're not house poor.

CHAPTER 20

Why You Can Borrow for Anything but Retirement.

Who wants to have enough money to retire right now? Everyone. How do we get there?

Here is an idea . . . why not just borrow the money you need to retire. Let's see, if you are going to live 20 more years, you will need $50,000 each year to cover all your living expenses. That comes out to a cool million dollars that you will need ($50,000 x 20 years = $1,000,000).

We are simplifying this example to make a point.

Now that you know you need $1,000,000, all you need now is someone to lend it to you. Head to any type of lender anywhere and explain what you would like to do.

"Hello, my name is (your name here). I'm here to inquire about a loan."

The lender responds by asking things like, "What is the purpose of the loan? What is the collateral? How will you repay it?" These are common sense questions that any lender will ask.

You explain, "Well, I want to retire. The purpose of the loan is to cover my retirement, which means I won't have any income to make payments from, except maybe a little Social security. I guess my retirement would also be the collateral."

The lender's response will be, "Ha!" Or maybe "Ha! Who put you up to this? This is a joke, right? Which of my friends sent you here?"

If that is not the lender's response, it should be. My point here is: you can borrow money for just about anything but retirement. No one will lend you money to retire.

Why not?

1. You don't have a source of income to repay the loan. If you did, you would not be borrowing money in the first place.

2. Retirement is like borrowing for a vacation - no one else can use it, resell it, or enjoy it, except for you. The value is only available to you. It has no collateral value. The difference with a vacation is that you go back to your source of income (your job) to repay the loan. When you retire, there is no source of income to which you can return.

That is why you can borrow money for just about anything *but* retirement.

CHAPTER 21

What Happens When Things Go Wrong?

Let's start with a few phrases or sayings you may have heard:

- There is never time to do it right. There is always time to do it over.
- First things first.
- It bothers me more that you did not admit your mistake than it does that you made a mistake.
- Oh, what a tangled web we weave when first we practice to deceive.
- The truth of the matter is that you always know the right thing to do. The hard part is doing it.
- I'm not upset that you lied to me. I'm upset that from now on I can't believe you.
- Better to offer no excuse than a poor one.
- Bad things happen to good people.
- If you want to make God laugh, tell him your plan for your life.

No matter how you say it, sometimes things go wrong. You don't plan for it, you don't expect it, and of course you don't like it.

What can go wrong in life? Here are just a few examples:

- You lose a job.
- Your house needs a new roof.
- You have a car accident.
- You suffer an Illness.
- Pay cut.

And there are more . . .

Let's just focus on the problem any of these situations can cause. You don't have enough money to make your loan payment. What do you do? You tell your lender you have a problem. You will not be able to make your payment or maybe not all of it. Don't make up excuses. Don't lie. Don't make promises you cannot keep.

Why?

Your lender can only help you if they understand your situation. They can only do that if you notify them early. Did you really think you could keep it from them? Believe me, once you miss a payment, they will know. Immediately. Remember, lenders track this stuff, and they are quite good at it.

What advantage is it to you? First, if they can, they will work with you on your payments by:

- Allowing you to pay interest only.
- Stretching out loan payments to reduce monthly amount due.
- Suspending payments for a short period of time.

Another important factor is that they can help you think through your situation and come up with ideas or solutions you did not consider.

What advantage is it to your lender? They do not want to own your house, car, or anything else for which you borrowed money. Remember, they are lenders, not owners or investors. Working with you to keep your car by modifying payments is in their best interest, too.

You might say, and you should say, "Hey, I have some legal rights and I want them to protect me." That is true, and they will, even if you tell them early. They cannot take away the laws in place that give you protections.

Finally, I would say that lenders are a lot like everyone else . . . including you. They will willingly work with those who work with them as best they can. They will also work with people who care. They will work with those that make the effort to pay their obligations and keep the promise made to repay money they borrowed.

I know. I have been there and done that with clients.

Things go wrong. When they do, you want people to be straight with you. You would help them if you could. When they don't tell you what's going on, how could you know how to help? Banks are in the same spot.

Let people help you.

You are more like a banker than you thought.

CHAPTER 22

Should All My Money Be in a Bank?

Should all your money be in a bank? Nope. By that I mean not all of your money should be in an insured bank account earning interest. Your money should be in the type of account most appropriate for its use.

Money you will need in about two years or less should be in an insured, stable bank account. You are going to need it in a short time, so it better be there when you need it. That's best served by an insured bank account.

What might you need this money for? Home down payment, car, wedding, etc. How bad would it be if you stuck some money you needed within two years in the stock market, and it dropped in value by 30%? That $10,000 you saved is now worth $7,000. You don't want to tell your loved one, "Sorry dear, but we can't get that house you like." That is not a conversation you want to have.

Money that has a very long-range need, like for retirement in 25 or 30 years or college tuition for a newborn child in 18 years, should be invested in some type of account that will provide a better long-term return. These alternatives are usually stock market based.

You can get these types of investments in mutual funds, 401(k)'s, IRAs, Roth IRAs, 529 plans, etc. If they drop in value one year, you have many years for them to recover. And they usually do. The rule of 72 plays a big part here.

Personally, I've lived through several huge market drops earlier in my life, when I was in my 20s, 30s and 40s. Things like the financial crisis of 2008-2013 or Black Monday, October 19, 1987, when the stock market fell by more than 22% in one day, are painful examples of this (yes, I do remember exactly where I was when I heard that news). This was the largest single-day drop EVER (so far). It is critical to allow time for them to recover. They always have.

It is very important that as you get closer to the day you need the money, you'll want to put it in something that is more stable, like a bank account. Why? Because you know you will need the money on a certain date. This is easier to do for a date-specific item like education, a home purchase or wedding. It is harder for something like retirement.

You don't need all your money for retirement on the first day of your retirement. With any luck, you'll be retired for a long time, hopefully for decades. So you'll always need some in stable funds and some in the market.

It's great to have money in the bank. It's better to have it where it works best for you.

CHAPTER 23

What is the Magic of Banking?

The Magic of Banking? Really? I have to be kidding, right? You mean, it's magic how you put your money in the bank and the bank charges you fees to access it, count it, and, then, *abracadabra*, they make money on my money by lending it to someone else? No, that is not what I mean.

Do I mean banks magically make your money disappear through mysterious fees?

No. This is not hocus-pocus.

What I mean by magic is the incredible amount of time and frustration your bank saves you in tracking, spending, saving, sending, receiving, counting, moving, converting, insuring, protecting and accessing your money.

You want to use your money, wherever, whenever, and however you want to use it. Instantly.

A bank makes that happen for you . . . like magic. Don't believe me? Does it sound too simple?

First, imagine if there were no banks. Where would you keep your money? Everyone says, "Under the mattress." Well if everyone kept money under their mattress, criminals would know where to look. There would be an epidemic of overturned mattresses.

Instead, you could put it in places no criminal would ever think to look, like cookie jars, freezers, dresser drawers, closets, kitchen cabinets, etc. These are all very original and secret (not). No one would ever think of looking in those or other "secret" hiding places for your money.

Here's a better idea – you could just carry all your money around with you. That way you would always have it, you couldn't possibly misplace it, you are not likely to be robbed, you can't be induced to waste it, and you certainly wouldn't lose it.

Let me ask you, how much money are you comfortable walking around with? You know, the amount that if you lost it, it would sting but it would not ruin your life. You would not be happy, but it was not your life's savings. Let's say it's about fifty bucks (and I'd still be upset if I lost it).

How much do you walk around with today? How much do you need to have so you always have enough for whatever comes up? Remember now, we are only talking about money in the form of cash.

So, if that is the way you are handling money, you will need to go to each business or person to whom you owe money in order to pay them. Here is a sample list:

Mortgage company or landlord (rent)

Cable TV

Cell phone

Electric

Gas

Home phone

Doctor

Dentist

Property Insurance

Newspaper

Property taxes

In addition, you need cash to purchase goods and services from:

Restaurants

Grocery stores

Gas stations

Auto mechanics

Hair or nail salons

Think of all the time you would be wasting by driving from place
to place to make your payments. You could save all that time if
you just sent cash through the mail. That makes sense. Not. Let's
just pretend I went on for a few pages about what a bad idea that is.
Don't forget the extra trips to the gas station (and cost) because of
all the driving you would be doing.

Ok, enough already. Who wants to do all that? Nobody. But wait,
you still say you don't need a bank. You don't have to do it all.
You could just ask a friend. Let's follow that thought.

Let's just say your friend's name is Pat. Or Kelly. It does not
matter. It could be your girl or guy friend. To have a friend replace
your bank you'll need to ask him or her to do the following: "Pat,
you're a good friend, and I trust you. I need you to do me a favor.
It's not all that complicated, but if it is something you are
uncomfortable with, feel free to say no."

Pat doesn't say no but he does not look too thrilled, either.

You plow on. "I need you to hold all of my money for me. Now
you can't tell anyone you have it (to protect my privacy), but you
will need to keep track of every penny I give you. I won't be
giving you the money all at one time; I will give it to you every
time I receive a paycheck or when someone gives me money.
There is going to be quite a bit of bookkeeping involved because of
all the additions."

Pat is starting to get that glazed-over look.

You keep going on, "Oh yeah, and you will have to keep track of
every penny I ask you to give someone else. Those would be the
subtractions. You see, I have lots of monthly obligations (rent,
electric, gas, phone, cable, internet . . .) that I need to pay. I guess

that is going to require more bookkeeping. And I might as well tell you, when it comes to my bookkeeping, you can never make a mistake. Hey, I'm relying on you. Remember I said I trust you. Are you okay with this, so far?"

Pat's replies, "So far? There's more?"

You answer, "I'm going to need you to keep a record of all incoming and outgoing transactions for about the last two years, so I can go back to that in case I need to prove I made a payment (more bookkeeping). In fact, as long as you are keeping track of everything, go ahead and send me a monthly statement showing all activity for me to review. On second thought, make it available to me on the Internet."

"And one more thing as it relates to bookkeeping, you will be paying me interest on some of my money, so I'll need a 1099 form at the end of the year so I can properly complete my income tax return. I think that's it on the bookkeeping."

"Pat, are you good so far?" Pat looks dazed and asks, "You want me to pay you interest and keep track of all of your money?"

You continue, "Now let's talk about how you will receive and send my money for me. First, you need to be able to receive money in person from me (in cash or check), but also via my phone, computer, wire, mail, or any other new technology that comes along. Receiving should be easy. Well, it will be if I have only one account type. I might want to have a few different accounts with different purposes: checking for transactions, savings for a rainy day, Christmas account for gifts, one in my name only, one jointly in my and my spouse's names. Guess that's gonna require more bookkeeping, monthly statements and 1099 forms, isn't it?"

Pat doesn't answer.

"But wait," you say, "there's more. Sending money is a little more complicated. While sending regular monthly payments via all the same methods as used for receiving money is easy, I'm going to need access to my money in any amount, at anytime, anywhere in the world. I can't tell you in advance where, when, how, the exact amount, or in what denomination I am going to ask you for it. It could be through my debit card at the local grocery store, or it could be in another state at an ATM, or it could be in a foreign country ATM."

You slap your forehead. "Wait, that brings up another issue… you will need to perform currency exchanges to any other country's currency from time to time. By the way, I am usually in a hurry, so you are going to need to get me my money, regardless of where I am, in about 30 seconds. I'm also going to be sending money by checks, phones, computers, wires, etc., all the same ways I receive it."

"Oh gosh, a key piece of holding my money is protecting it. First, you'll need to protect it from robbers, thieves, and muggers. However, since we are also moving money over the Internet, you'll need to protect it from cyber-criminals, too. Piece of cake."

"In addition to protecting it from criminals of all kinds, I need you to insure it, but only up to $250,000 per account. I think you would want that protection too, wouldn't you? I mean who doesn't want their money insured in case the person holding it goes broke or disappears. And to prevent that from happening, you will be subject to an annual audit by an accounting firm and regular examinations by governmental regulatory bodies like the FDIC and the State Department of Financial Institutions. "

"Okay Pat, that covers most everything, at least for starters. I just want to say one more time though that you can't tell anyone you are doing this for me, my privacy is really important, and there are laws that protect me from your misuse of my information and likely penalize you for doing so."

What do you think Pat's answer will be to your request of a favor? Remember, you told Pat it was okay to say no. After you gave Pat smelling salts, he would think you were crazy.

Here is the real magic of banking: Open an account with a bank to handle all your transactions. You can bring in money in person, mail it in, send it in via wire, phone, or computer or really any legal means possible. They'll accept it. Heck, they'll even count it when it's in cash to ensure it is the correct amount. By the way, the person counting it will have someone watching them to make sure they get it right or that there is no stealing and they will be on camera . . . ahhh, security.

Banks protect your money from all criminals, cyber and otherwise, and insure via the FDIC (yes, banks pay for that insurance) up to $250,000 per separate account title should the bank cease to exist.

You can have access to your money at anytime, anywhere via nearly any means, and they will deliver cash into your hands anywhere in the world within about 30 seconds. They will account for every penny and provide you with monthly statements of your activity, historical records for a couple of years, and any necessary tax reporting forms. They are bound by the terms of their privacy agreement and are subject to annual audits and regulatory examinations.

Banks do all that for you and your money – all according to government regulations. Ask yourself who in their right mind would accept that responsibility and not get paid to do so? Just having an accountant keep track of your transactions will cost you more than $100/hour. Think about how much that would cost you per month. The fact is, when it comes to your money, banks provide you tremendous security, accuracy, access, integrity, consistency, and flexibility. All of this is at little to no cost to you.

Voilá! That, my friends, is the magic of banking. And why everyone should be using a bank to handle their money.

CONCLUSION

There are no dumb questions about money.

The end is really just the beginning.

I hope I helped you better understand money. More importantly, this book helped you to understand your money: where it is, where it's going, how it's going, how to keep track of it (and how your bank does it for you), and mostly, how not to let it leave you without you knowing it.

There are no dumb questions about money.

When it comes to money, no surprises are a good thing. Simple things are easy for me to understand. When things are explained to me in simple terms, I get it. The mark of a truly intelligent person is one who can really help you understand something that is complex by explaining it to you in simple, clear, easy-to-understand language.

From complex to simple. From buzzwords to believability. It's my money. I know where it is. I get it. And I can get it. That is simply brilliant.

This law of simplicity applies to anything: medical, financial, technology, family, business, and more. You name it, and the law of simplicity works best.

Money is like a meniscus. Sound complicated? It's not.

When I developed a recurring soreness in my knee, I consulted an orthopedic surgeon. He did an excellent job of explaining my knee and its problem in really simple terms. Based on his significant medical schooling and training, he could have launched into the following description:

"The meniscus is a crescent-shaped structure composed of cartilage that functions to distribute body weight evenly across the three bones that make up the knee joint: the thigh bone, shin bone, and knee cap. The surfaces of these bones are covered with cartilage, which allows the bones to move smoothly against each other without causing damage to the bone."

Thankfully, he didn't do that to me. My knee hurt. I didn't need my head to hurt, too.

Instead, he skipped all that and said to me, "your knee is like an Oreo. The wafers of the cookie represent your bones. The soft creme (crème is Oreo-lingo for cream) filling between your wafers is your meniscus. The creme filling keeps your knee working smoothly, without pain."

Which description do you understand better? Which would you be able to remember and use to describe to a friend five years from now when they are complaining about knee pain?

Would you recommend this doctor?

So why did my meniscus cause me pain? He told me it was torn, and that a tear in a meniscus is like a having a hang nail. It's annoying. It won't go away until you clip it off. "That's what we'll do in a surgery - we'll clip off the torn part."

I was relieved. Even though I still had to go through the surgery, I completely understood my knee, the problem with my knee and how it would be repaired. I'm guessing you do, too. Pretty simple. Pretty brilliant.

I do hope that I have done the same with money by explaining it in clear and simple terms. From this book, you should now understand what form of money to use, when to use it, and how to avoid wasting it on interest and fees that give you no value.

The purpose of this book was to help you understand money. What's happening to your money, where it's going, who is taking it, and how to be smart about using it.

Remember, nobody cares about your money more than you. Banks come (selfishly) close, but even banks can't stop you from being careless. You have to care. If you could not care less, then finding your money will always be a mystery to you.

This book makes it easy for you know how to care about, and for, your money. If you really want to learn more about balancing checkbooks, creating budgets, calculating interest costs on loans and credit cards, and many other money-related subjects, you should seek out books, websites, videos, classes and more that will teach you how to do those things.

This stuff is not hard to find and most of it is free. The access to the information does not discriminate. There is a wealth of free information that is available to anyone who wants to learn it. You do have to invest your time.

I hope you do because that means you are really on your way.

Banks can help, too. They aren't just vaults with money. It could be argued that the real value a bank will provide is through people you can trust. Remember, banks need you to make good financial decisions. Their success counts on it. When someone else has skin in the game, it's a good thing. You need them. They need you. Simple.

Don't expect that people who are trying to sell you something will put your interest first. When someone is trying to sell you something, your interest probably is not ranked as high as their own.

This is true for two reasons: First, if they are paid when they sell something, they want to sell you something. There's nothing wrong with this. You just have to realize it.

Second, how can you be sure they understand money any more than you do?

If they have not read this book, it's likely that you know money better than they do. Why would you expect someone who sells TVs to understand finance? Hopefully they understand TV technology and can advise you on one that is good for you. It is unlikely the salesperson is an expert on what form of money to use, and which one is most cost effective for you to use. That is up to you.

From reading this book, you should be able to make a good money decision the next time, and the next time, and the next time.

You have to want it. You have to want more than money… you have to want to understand money.

You can be brilliant about money. You should already feel relief because you get it. Now go get it.

And ask questions.

EPILOGUE

Remember, no one cares as much about your money as you. Ask questions and don't worry what others might think. It's your money, and there are no dumb questions about it.

Now you understand money . . . probably a lot more than others do. Along with the understanding, you know how to better care for it. A good bank can be your good friend. They understand money and how to care for it.

There are several tools available to help you move your money, and maybe even hold some of it. The ever-growing list includes PayPal, BitCoin, mobile phone apps, internet banking, Apple Pay, Google wallet, TransferWise, Square Cash, Popmoney, Western Union and stored value cards. More are being developed every day. You should use all the tools available to you to move your money, but hold it in a bank.

None of these products are designed to help you better understand money. They exist to move your money faster (and I hope securely) from you to another. That means they are designed to help you spend your money faster. And, they do it to earn a fee. The fee comes from you, the person you are sending it to, the merchant, or someone else in the chain of the money flow. Companies are built to generate revenue and profit, not to provide products and services for free.

It helps banks to help you understand money. Do they charge for some of their services? Yes, just as other service providers do. Sometimes the fee comes from you, and sometimes it comes from another point in the money flow. Banks also pay you for the use of your money, and share their expertise with you, which helps you even more. That's a pretty good deal.

Remember these simple facts:

- Banks pay to insure your money for you while they hold it.
- Banks keep track of lots of money for people and companies.

- The government regulates and examines banks.
- Banks are required to have an accounting firm audit them.

If you are thinking about having someone else hold your money for you, ask them if they will do everything a bank does. And if they say yes, ask them if they are monitored and regulated like a bank.

To be clear . . . *there are no dumb questions about money . . . especially if it's yours.*

BONUS QUESTION

As a bonus for reading the book, you get an extra smart question about money . . .

BONUS SMART QUESTION: What If Money Falls Into Your Retirement Fund?

If a tree falls in the forest and no one is there to hear it, does it make any noise?

If money automatically comes out of your paycheck and goes into an account for you, did you ever really miss it?

The best way to save money is to never let it pass through your hands. If it does, it usually pauses and looks around for something to spend itself on.

Do you know how much money you spend on federal income taxes? State income taxes? Social Security? Not likely. Check your pay stub sometime (electronic or paper). You will be surprised how much money you don't keep. The reason the government does not let you keep all your money and write them a check for your taxes at year end is because they know most people will not have the money to pay their taxes when they are due.

They don't even know when or if you will retire, but that does not stop them from taking your money from you for your own retirement.

You should have the same attitude. Don't rely on you to write yourself a check for your retirement account, vacation account, children education account, etc. Likely, you will have used the money for something else; either on purpose, or you simply forgot that you need to save some money. Even more likely, you figure you will start saving with the next paycheck.

Have money taken out of your paycheck for retirement, from your first paycheck. Don't even wait to see how much your checks will be before you decide how much to save. The government is not waiting until they know how much you owe them or for you to tell them when you will retire . . . they simply start collecting. From the start. You should do the same. And, you don't have to limit yourself to doing this for retirement. Do it with anything you want to save for. Ask to have it taken out of your paycheck and directly deposited to your account. You'll be glad you did, especially at retirement. You can't borrow money for retirement.

ABOUT THE AUTHOR

Joe Fazio is Co-founder, Board Chairman and CEO of Commerce State Bank in West Bend, Wisconsin. He currently serves on the Board of Directors for the Federal Home Loan Bank of Chicago and has served on the Board of Directors of the Wisconsin Bankers Association. Joe is a 1983 graduate of St. Norbert College (B.A. Business Administration), and in 1988 earned his MBA from Edgewood College.

Joe regularly speaks on the importance of understanding money. His audiences appreciate his entertaining, common sense approach and the fact that while he talks about money and banks, Joe does not sound banker-ish.

CPSIA information can be obtained
at www.ICGtesting.com
Printed in the USA
LVOW07s1326111017
552026LV00014B/416/P